# The
# *Rhetoric*
# of
# *Humanism:*
## *Spanish Culture*
## *after*
## *Ortega y Gasset*

Thomas Mermall

¿Ω Ψ Φ Σ ?
¿Ψ Φ Σ Θ ?
¡Φ Σ Θ Υ !

# The
# *R*hetoric
# of
# *H*umanism:
# Spanish Culture
# after
# Ortega y Gasset

# *Bilingual Press/Editorial Bilingüe*

## Studies in the Literary Analysis of Hispanic Texts

**Address:**

**Editorial**
Bilingual Press
Department of Foreign Languages
York College, CUNY
Jamaica, New York  11451
212-969-4047/4035

**Business**
Bilingual Press
552 Riverside Drive  Suite 1-B
New York, New York 10027
212-866-4595

# *The*
# *Rhetoric*
# *of*
# *Humanism:*
# *Spanish Culture*
# *after*
# *Ortega y Gasset*

*Thomas Mermall*

¿ Ω Ψ Φ Σ ?
¿ Ψ Φ Σ Θ ?
¡ Φ Σ Θ Υ !

ISBN: 0-91650-02-6

*Printed in the United States of America*

# Acknowledgments

Chapter I of this study first appeared in *Bulletin of Hispanic Studies,* (January, 1973). I wrote the rest of the text expressly for this book.

Thematic and methodological exigencies in Chapter IV made it necessary and practical to deviate slightly from the consistent foot-note logic found in other chapters.

For helpful comments I owe many thanks to colleagues and friends who read portions of the manuscript: Professors Donald W. Bleznick, Robert M. Levine, Edmund L. King, Gonzalo Sobejano, Philip W. Silver, and Richard M. Zaner. Special thanks to Miss Patricia Connell for typing the manuscript. I alone am responsible the contents.

In the course of writing this book I benefited from the works and stimulating company of Thomas Altizer, and found inspiration in the exemplary humanism of Dr. Edmund D. Pellegrino. My deepest gratitude to both for their support and encouragement.

*For*
Robert G. Mead Jr.,
*in gratitude and friendship*

# Table of Contents

*Introduction*                                                    1

## PART ONE
## CONSERVATIVE HUMANISM

*I. Esthetics and Politics in Falangist Culture
(1935-1945)*                                                     17

*II. Laín Entralgo and the Topics of Humanism*                   27

  1. Humanistic Discourse: Models, Examples, Formu-
    las                                                        27

      The dignity of belief                                  30
      What is Humanism?                                      32
      The vocation of being human                            34

  2. Humanism and Politics                                      36

      Background: The experience of the Civil War            36
      The topics of Humanism                                 40
      A reply to *Huis Clos*                                 41
      Laín and Camus                                         42
      Leisure                                                44

  3. The Rhetoric of Conservative Humanism                      45

      Friendship and politics                                47
      Conclusion: Laín and Teilhard de Chardin               49

*III. Psychoanalysis and Culture: Creative My-
thology in the Work of Juan Rof Carballo*                        53

      Freud in Spain, an outline                             53
      The work of Juan Rof Carballo                          57
      Method                                                 58

1. Anthropology    59

     The biological model    59
     The mythical model: a Promethean interpretation of the Oedipus legend    62
     A historicist interpretation    64
     Displacement of the super-ego    64
     The hermeneutics of restoration    68
     Language and silence    71

2. Myth as Rhetoric    72

     Paradox as drama and wisdom    72
     The negative example of Prometheus-Oedipus    73
     Myth as rhetoric    75
     The uses of analogy    76
     Rof's imagery    77
     The function of the image    79
     Conclusion    80

# PART TWO
# SOCIALIST HUMANISM

*IV. The New Humanism*    85

1. Enrique Tierno Galván: Reality, Control, Happiness    85

2. Reality as Result    88

3. The Rhetoric of Anti-Humanism    92

     The esthetic sensibility    92
     Literary terminology as rhetoric    94
     Definitions and allusions    95
     The language of provocation    96
     The anti-topics    97
     Style and thought: the dialectical function of the essay    101
     Tierno and Socialism    104
     Conclusion    106

*V. José Luis Aranguren and the Role of the Moralist in Our Time*    108

     Practical ethics    110
     Awakening the Spanish Catholics    110

    Humanism and humanitarianism 111
    Communication and the illusion of happiness 112
    A lexicon of realities 113
    One step to the left: Carlos Castilla del Pino as
      moralist 114

*Conclusion* 117

*Notes* 121

*Bibliography* 130

    English translations of original works 130

    A selected critical bibliography of the contemporary
      Spanish essay and the history of ideas 130

    General bibliography 132

# INTRODUCTION

This book is a study of the dominant ideas in Spanish culture since the Civil War of 1936 and an analysis of the figurative language and forms of argument that express them. I have centered my inquiry not on systematic thought or philosophy as a technical discipline, but rather on the general intellectual and moral concerns of a generation of thinkers—specifically, the images of man and concepts of society and culture.

The vehicle for the expression of these ideas is primarily the essay. This literary genre often conveys concepts which the writer may have explained in a systematic fashion in a more extensive piece of work, or which he hopes to formulate at length in the future. Unlike formal philosophical expositions, the essay communicates concepts in a synthetic, economic and urgent manner, and as such is most suitable to express theory in a language understandable to the non-specialist with a humanistic education. This does not mean that the function of the essay is necessarily to popularize ideas but rather to dramatize them. In modern Spanish letters a remarkable example of this dramatization is found in Ortega y Gasset, whose enthusiasm for ideas has been appreciated by his disciples as "the adventure of our intelligence and sensibility."[1] Indeed, the term adventure is very apt, for it captures so many of the qualities of Ortega's essays: an intellectual daring conveyed in a vigorous and flamboyant style, the markedly exploratory structure of so many of his essays, and above all, the notion of existence as continual risk and drama. Because for Ortega man is not only a thinking being but also a *res dramatica*, both in his resolve to live authentically through the pursuit of his vocation and in his response to circumstances.[2] This means, among other things, that intellectual activity—i.e., the experience of reality as a problem and the search for truth—the essay, a genre he cultivated with singular success, was a means of dramatizing his intellectual mission.

The notion of drama can be useful in defining the essay as a genre. When Juan Marichal describes it as literary form in which the writer seeks to relate to his socio-historical world, he is implicitly assigning the essay a unique capacity to express the tensions between writer and society.[3] Of course, often the intellectual's response to his circumstances is inauthentic, as Ortega well saw. That is, he does not come to grips with the cultural imperatives of his time, either because of self-imposed limitations or because, as the early post war years in

Spain would indicate, censorship and intellectual isolation reduced severely the necessary tensions that make culture a drama. Under such conditions dramatic substance is replaced by mere gesture or pose, the cliché is passed off for originality and the essay loses its polemical spirit. For, as the examples of Montaigne and Bacon remind us, it is precisely out of a confrontation with official science and philosophy that the essay evolved as a genre, and for this reason Theodor W. Adorno described it as a "skepticism of method" and a "critique of ideology."[4] To the German critic the essay is an open form of criticism which affirms a partial, ephemeral and historical truth. It would seem here that Adorno is contradicting Marichal's idea of the essay, for in affirming a partial truth against absolute values the writer is differentiating himself from, not relating to, society. But the opposition is more apparent than real. Whether the essayist affirms or negates a given ideology he does so nevertheless through a partial truth that is either associated with or related to an absolute value, or, as Adorno suggests, it is dissociated from a total view in which case the function of the essay is dialectical.

Obviously, other genres such as the novel can also convey this tension between the writer and his society, but the essay, being a more conscious and deliberate expression of theory, conveys ideas with a sense of urgency, immediacy and intensity, with an emphasis on man in his socio-historical setting. Moreover, the essayist wishes to dramatize ideas not as fictions or subjective states of consciousness, but as facts, not as symbols but as concrete events. As J. Giordano has observed, "the authentic essayist does not seek to express the confused realities of his interiority, but to participate to the extent that it is possible in a truth which he (obviously) holds to be objective. . .The essay consequently can be defined as a non-fictitious epic in which the objectivity of the world and of ideas is not symbolic but real."[5] To speak of the essay as an "epic of the intellect" is only another way of stressing the essentially dramatic function of the genre.

The fact that the essayist considers the world of ideas as facts does not mean that he employs exclusively the impersonal, objective, technical language of formal disciplines. The essay as expression of theory, and especially as a method of demonstration, consists of predominantly subjective, imaginative, implicit proofs. However, the essayist also depends necessarily, but to a limited degree, on formal proofs based on logical necessity. Following up the idea of the dramatic function of the essay it would seem that a tension between subjective and objective modes of discourse is an intrinsic formal element of this genre. Whereas the novelist can employ, exclusively, either a subjective or objective form of narration, the genuine essayist normally oscillates between a logical-discursive language that affirms the objective validity of his thesis, and an imaginative, suasory or figurative language that compensates for the lack of explicit proof. To remain within the bounds of the genre the essay cannot fall either into total subjectivism (lyricism) or lapse into total objectivity (formal discourse). Rather, it must mantain a tension or interdependence between the autonomous, logical sequence of concepts and the personal experience and impression of those concepts; its structure therefore is based on the interdependence of observation and introspection, intuition and logic, imagination and intellect, implicit and explicit proofs.

The restrictions and limitations that the essayist imposes on his topic and the synthetic, condensed nature of his expression of theory reduce the possibility of explicit proof in the progression of argument. By explicit proof I mean the methodical, consistent development of an argument or thesis based either on objectively verifiable data or on logical necessity. But the brevity and economy of exposition are not the decisive factors in reducing the possibility of explicit proof. The distinctive characteristic of the essay as an instrument of theoretical proof seems to be what C. Morón Arroyo has called "discontinuous demonstration:" arguments based on arbitrary, unexpected, intuitive transitions from premises to conclusions.[6] The fact that the essay is concerned less with distinctions, differentiations and logical progression and more with condensation and unification gives the genre an essentially rhetorical tenor. Hence, Ortega's apt definition of the essay as "science minus the explicit proof."[7] This idea of discontinuous demonstration applies not only to conventional essays but also to longer works such as Unamuno's *Tragic Sense of Life* or to give a contemporary example, Rof Carballo's *Violence and Tenderness* which abound with rhetorical proofs. Since a good number of the works considered in this study are of monographic length yet retain the traits of the essay, it would be more convenient to speak of "essayistic discourse" which includes both standard essays and longer pieces. A few thinkers and artists, notably Laín Entralgo and Torrente Ballester (Chapters I, II) have also expressed their views in the form of plays, which are also examined.

In the essay-type of discourse the subjective, personal dimension of the work should be discernible, and this factor is worth isolating

3

only if the tropes or forms of argument are to some extent unusual, unique or highly suggestive. The genuine essay in addition to providing information also conveys an esthetic emotion and this is true of the longer expositions that fall into what I call "essayistic discourse." In other words, the essay is characterized by a certain tone, style, or personal manner. The rhetorical analysis in the following chapters does not consist of diagraming or cataloguing tropes and forms of argument, but rather entails an attempt to isolate the primary rhetorical figures of thought that define the intellectual perspective of each individual essayist. In some cases I have determined the root metaphor which illustrates the author's basic theme. Or, I have sought the "objective correlative" to a rich analogy whose terms correspond not only to the inmediate context but to an "extrinsic order of motivation"[8] (as Kenneth Burke would say) implicit in the writer's *Weltanschauung*.

There remains the need to classify the various types of essay, a task already undertaken by such critics as Robert G. Mead and Jorge Mañach. Mead offers a literary spectrum of the essay ranging from the most objective modes (treatise, monograph) to the most subjective (sketches and esquisses). He also differentiated the essay from the article, the critical study and the monograph, all of which approximate the essay.[9] Mañach further classifies the essay according to its thematic emphases or *acentos;* thus the essay can be philosophical, socio-historical, cultural, critical, didactic, or poetic.[10] *Of all these it is the philosophical and the cultural essay that is of primary interest here* and it is appropiate for the purposes of this study to classify these into two main categories suggested by E. Tierno Galván: the esthetic and the critical.[11] The esthetic essay does not resist or oppose the reality it describes but is content to comprehend and appreciate a particular aspect of culture. Its ultimate objective is to induce contemplation of ideas relatively free from historical contingencies. The critical essay addresses directly the dominant ideas of a historical moment; it reflects a consciousness bent on a reevaluation or subversion of values through a critique of ideology. The esthetic essay as an instrument of culture is the expression of the intellectual's concern with the compatibility of values. The critical essay on the other hand is an instrument of negation of the existing institutions.

For at least fifteen years after the Civil War only the esthetic essay was cultivated in Spain. In the late 1950s, with the gradual relaxation of censorship, there emerged among some writers a relatively critical

4

attitude, and at the beginning of the new decade with the appearence of Enrique Tierno Galván's *Desde el espectáculo a la trivialización* (1961) the liberals (most of them Orteguians and Christian Democrats) came under the gradual indirect challenge of socialist and Marxist thinkers. But the undeclared polemic did not center around concrete socio-political problems, a type of encounter the regime would not permit. It became, rather, a conflict of total views of the nature of man, society and culture. In other words, the post-Civil War essay became for the most part the expression of a conflict of humanisms: an opposition between those who, like Pedro Laín Entralgo and Juan Rof Carballo, wish to reconcile traditional values grounded in religious belief with secular culture, and those who, like Enrique Tierno Galván and Carlos Castilla del Pino, want to create new values derived from the social sciences. I have labeled these two attitudes conservative humanism and socialist humanism respectively.

The term humanism is applied to the essayists grouped together in this study because they have successfully related the import of their respective disciplines to anthropological and ethical questions. Furthermore, all have given considerable attention to the topic of humanism: Aranguren's *Sobre el humanismo,* Tierno's *Humanismo y sociedad,* and Castilla's *El humanismo imposible,* to mention only a few. Although I discuss the various meanings and contexts of the term humanism in the forthcoming chapters, a few introductory remarks are in order.

In contemporary Spanish literature the essay has achieved an artistic merit comparable only to that of poetry. Unamuno, Ortega and Machado not only raised it to new heights of literary excellence but also employed it as a medium for philosophical speculation. All three had a humanistic orientation inasmuch as the substance of their work is addressed to the problem of human existence. But the high esthetic and intellectual caliber of the contemporary Spanish essay can also be attributed to the cultural sophistication and artistic talent of the medical humanists whose literary and critical works constitute an exceptional phenomenon in modern Spanish letters. Cajal, Marañón, Novoa-Santos, Martí-Ibáñez are probably the most familiar. Cajal, the Nobel laureate in neurophysiology, is associated with the generation of 1898. Like his contemporaries, he ventured into the history of ideas and literary criticism with *La psicología del Quijote...*(1905). Marañón, a member of Ortega's generation, wrote psychological analyses of Don Juan, the paintings of El Greco and the personal life of Amiel. The intellectual tradition of the medical humanist continues in Spain to this day and it is no exaggeration to say that some of that country's best thinkers are men of letters trained in medicine.

In view of this eminent tradition two chapters of this book deal with the work of medical humanists. Laín and Rof follow in the tradition of Cajal and Marañón in that they complement and enrich scientific knowledge with philosophical speculation. Both have developed a personalist concept of medicine based on the notion that man, more than an *object* of scientific inquiry, is primarily a *person* whose ultimate identity is rooted in his freedom and selfhood *(intimidad)*.

The humanist's recourse to disciplines ancillary to his own goes beyond an interest in effective and thorough method; it responds to the essentially ethical motivation for his search for knowledge. For men like Laín and Rof science achieves its most fully human function in society when its theoretical premises are tested in the context of such questions as "What is man?" and "What constitutes his ultimate good?" A further implication of this attitude is intellectual tolerance. The humanist abhors discord; above all, he wishes to understand the other point of view and establish a dialogue with men of different persuasions. Harmony and compatibility, therefore, are central tenets of *traditional* humanism. Thus, Laín titles a collection of essays *Ejercicios de comprensión,* and in his classic study *España como problema* he avers that "in the Spain that I envision there can and should co-exist Cajal and Juan Belmonte, the heritage of Saint Ignatius and the estimation of Unamuno, the thought of Saint Thomas and that of Ortega."[12] The humanist also has a strong sense of pedagogical mission. "What I have accepted as my task," writes Aranguren, "is to help Spanish Catholics to free themselves from the narrowness of their Catholicism; Marxists from the dogmatism of their views; and likewise the other groups, democrats, Christians, Falangists. . .I have excluded no one as my interlocutor."[13]

Tierno Galván and Castilla del Pino, who have a dialectical concept of culture, are not concerned with the ethics of compatibility or with the reconciliation of traditional and modern values. By negating the present image of society and simultaneously affirming totally a scientific method of social knowledge, they await the emergence of a new humanism. For Tierno any philosophy that emphasizes the subjectivity, individuality or grandeur of man must be rejected, for only when man is defined first as a social being can we expect a genuine humanism. Similarly, Castilla rejects a personalist ethic in the name of a dialectical anthropology.

The essays of Tierno are an outright challenge of the premises of both religious and non-religious Spanish humanism. As a philosopher of praxis Tierno opposes the notion so dear to Unamuno, Machado and Ortega that reality has to be *invented*. Although Ortega was very much in favor of precision in thought and the need to respond to the primacy of concrete reality, he still felt that the task of the philosopher was to *seduce* the reader to see things in a certain way. Tierno attributes to invention and seduction, or the "literary mentality" as he calls it, a negative value. Literary dramatization of ideas, therefore, is for him a pseudo-philosophy because it is a product of the imagination and not of analysis. Of course, Tierno himself relies on a "literary intelligence" not to formulate philosophical theories, but as an instrument of negation in the form of the essay. Without mentioning his contemporaries by name Tierno's critique of traditional humanism in post-Civil War Spain is implacable and corrosive.

If the two kinds of humanisms discussed above have anything in common it is a desire to eliminate what their exponents consider inhuman forms of existence, whether they be found in the misapplication and tyranny of technology (Laín, Rof) or in the alienated modes of interpersonal relations rooted in capitalism (Tierno, Castilla).

As the title suggests, this book is both an inquiry into the kinds of humanism in contemporary Spain and a study of the *rhetoric* of humanism. It is then, an exercise in both intellectual history and literary analysis. But what precisely is the relation between rhetoric and humanism? If we accept the definition of humanism to be essentially an ethic, that is, the expression of particular values, then rhetoric is an inseparable element of humanistic discourse. When one hears that existentialism or Marxism "is a humanism" the implications are that we are not merely being asked to accept a collection of empirical data about man and the cosmos nor even a tightly reasoned, formal theory. Humanism, as a philosophy, attitude or program for the improvement of mankind, is an appeal to values whose ultimate justification is grounded not in reason but belief. In other words, whereas explicit demonstration and logical inference in discourse can only prove specific intellectual propositions, implicit, ethical (rhetorical) proof appeals to the richness, the totality of an individual's experience.

7

The humanist is a fervent believer in the efficacy of persuasion. Like Plato and the Renaissance men of letters before them, Laín and Rof, for example, find a necessary interdependence between dialectical argumentation which seeks to demonstrate the truth of a proposition by an appeal to reason, and a rhetorical demonstration which attempts to persuade by an appeal to the emotions. Whereas the object of dialectical reasoning is impersonal—objective truth sought with arguments capable of enlisting the assent of any reasonable man—the object of suasory discourse is to appeal to man's moral dispositions. Since rhetoric, unlike dialectic, is not concerned primarily with facts or correct reasoning but with man's *potentiality for the good* (Plato, Aristotle), it operates in the realm of the possible and the desirable.[14] Rhetoric, then as *deloûn* (to make one see) and as *psykhagogein* (to direct the soul) is an art in the service of the good, and when it complements reason it becomes the expression of the philosopher's enthusiasm for truth.[15]

The mode of demonstration proper to rhetoric is the enthymeme. The enthymeme is to rhetoric what the syllogism is to logic, except that the former moves from probable premises to probable conclusions. Hence, as a form of proof it must compensate for logical certainty with imaginative reasoning. In the context of ethics, the rhetorical argument is the exploitation of human potential. If one admits, then, that humanism is essentially a concept of man as possibility (as vocation, Ortega would say) then rhetoric is an intrinsic element of humanistic discourse.

The present study is divided into two main sections: Conservative Humanism and Socialist Humanism. Chapter One is a prelude to the theme of conservative humanism. It deals with some aspects of literature in Spain during the Civil War and shows how geometry and architecture—symbols of the Fascist state—are the central imagery in the rhetoric of Falangism.

Chapter Two, an analysis of the essays of Laín Entralgo, introduces some of the basic motifs in Christian humanism: the rhetorical *admiratio* of the grandeur of man, a search for the synthesis between reason and faith and the interdependence of ethics and politics. Special attention is given to Laín's notion that secularism is a deformation or aberration of an eternal, spiritual hierarchical model of man and the cosmos, and to his concept of truth as "recapitulation of knowledge." Furthermore, Laín's humanistic politics, expressed in his plays, is compared to Camus' *Les Justes*.

Chapter Three explores the function of myth in the work of Juan Rof Carballo, especially his use of symbolic personification, paradox and arguments *ad hominem* to dramatize the loss of traditional values and the erosion of present institutions.

Chapter Four begins the study of Socialist humanism with an explication and rhetorical analysis of Tierno Galván's subversive language. This chapter concentrates on unusual definitions, the use of aphorisms, the negative meaning of literary terminology, the dissociation of concepts and the dialectical function of the essay.

The last chapter defines the role of the moralist in Spanish letters with an examination of the works of José Luis Aranguren, a progressive Catholic, and Carlos Castilla del Pino, a Marxist.

Since the first two chapters contain considerable information about post-Civil War culture, I will here make only some general observations on the intellectual life of that period.

When Ortega returned to Madrid in 1945 after some ten years of absence, he found the Spanish cultural climate inhospitable to the spirit of his philosophy. Intellectual life was anything but a sense of drama; it was rather, at least from 1939-50, closer to what Tierno has called a "culture of hibernation." The end of the Civil War meant to the majority of the victors the continuation on an ideological plane of a crusade against the vestiges of a secular, liberal and heterodox "anti-Spain." Under such conditions Ortega's presence did little to reanimate Spanish letters. His contributions to the Instituto de Humanidades, which he founded with Julián Marías in 1948, fell short of raising Spanish thought to a meaningful level. In poor health, disillusioned with politics and intimidated by the authorities, Ortega eschewed repeated requests from his disciples to assume the intellectual leadership of the new generation.

A partial break with official intolerance and the beginnings of a semblance of intellectual activity were initiated by the liberal Falangists with the publication of the journal *Escorial* (1940-50). In the very first issue, the editors, Laín Entralgo and the poet and former minister of propaganda, Dionisio Ridruejo, declared their desire to relax ideological tensions and gradually bring an end to the prevalent manichean view of Spanish history. *Escorial*'s objectives were modest: to elevate the literary and philosophical standards in Spanish letters with the collaboration of such figures as Menéndez Pidal, Baroja, Rosales and Zubiri. In their genuine desire to counteract the crusading spirit of neotraditionalist fanatics and integrate all cultur-

9

al values, the editors would, from time to time, bring back to the fold intellectuals or poets held in official disrepute. Thus, after a ritual reprimand for his "political foolishness" the poet Antonio Machado would be "rescued" as a great poetic spirit.

The core of liberal Falangism consisted of Laín, Ridruejo, Tovar, Rosales, Vivanco and Torrente Ballester. All are associated with the generation of 1936, as all are born between 1907 and 1913. In its full sense this designation also includes the emigrés, or as Manuel Durán has observed, all those spiritually wounded by the experience of the Civil War.[16] But in the Peninsular context the label "generation of '36" means two things. First it refers to the above-named Falangists who, in 1938, were united in a common political and cultural cause and who subsequently determined the direction of post-Civil War intellectual life. Unlike other Fascist groups, the liberal Falangists were inclined toward the ideological flexibility of their founder José Antonio Primo de Rivera and the philosophy of Ortega y Gasset.

Secondly, the generation of '36 refers to what Julián Marías has called a "complementary constellation:" writers who coexist publicly with the first group and may even share some of their views, but whose difference in age, intellectual formation and general outlook sets them apart as a separate group.[17] Names like Zubiri, Menéndez Pidal, Aranguren, G. Díaz-Plaja, and Marías would be peripheral to the generation of '36.

The neotraditionalist intellectuals of the period refused to identify themselves with the generation of '36. One of their spokesmen, Vicente Marrero, called the group "the minority of 1948," which under the leadership of Rafael Calvo-Serer organized most of its activities around the journal *Arbor,* the center known as Consejo Superior de Investigaciones Científicas and the Catholic lay organization of the Opus Dei. According to Marrero the basic disagreement between the generation of '36 and the minority of '48 was based on a difference of attitudes concerning the purpose of the Civil War. "For us," avers Marrero, "it was a war between those who wished to preserve their faith in God and those without God; between the cross and the red star; between intelligence and the 'intelligentsia'; a struggle between being and nothingness."[18]

The Marxist Socialist thinkers do not fit too readily into the generation of '36. Tierno Galván, the oldest of these Socialists was born in 1916, studied under the former Falangist Montero Díaz and was for a time a Monarchist. But Tierno's work is practically antithetical to the position of the generation of '36, for he has reversed the function of the intellectual in society by attacking systematically the most cherished beliefs of the group. Armed with the analytic tools of Neo-positivism and Marxism, Tierno launched in 1954 a new approach in the study of society with the publication of his monthly *Boletín informativo,* which lasted until 1964.

Castilla del Pino, who was born in 1922 began reading Marx at the age of thirty-four and belongs to the new generation of young Marxists who began to surface in the early 1960s: Manuel Ballesteros, Manuel Sacristán, Elías Díaz and Francisco Fernández Santos. Ballesteros' work *Marx o la crítica como fundamento* (Ed. Ciencia Nueva, 1967), is a rich and complex study of the idea of negativity in dialectical reason and its historical link to the existentialism of Kierkegaard and Sartre. Fernández Santos in a series of essays collected in *Historia y filosofía; ensayos de dialéctica* (Madrid: Península, 1966) has defended Marxism as a critical theory against those who have emphasized its strictly economic, deterministic and dogmatic expressions. For Fernández Santos, Marxism is a "realistic humanism."

While the '40s were, as Martín Santos said, "years of silence," the early '50s were in a narrow sense polemical years. The liberal Catholic sector was attempting to settle once and for all the dispute about "the problem of Spain" with the neotraditionalists. Topics of the day included the explications of Heideggerian and Orteguian texts, accompanied by Catholic apologetics inspired by the anthropology of Xavier Zubiri, and dissertations on the "essence of Spain." There were, however, noteworthy intellectual contributions such as Aranguren's study of Protestantism and Laín's biological and phenomenological analysis of expectation and hope.

The '60s saw a considerable relaxation of censorship. Journals such as the *Revista de Occidente* and *Cuadernos para el diálogo* provided a forum for ideas. Books dealing with Marxist and existentialist themes, unavailable since the Civil War, were now sold openly. There also emerged a group of socially conscious and committed clergymen inspired by Vatican II, and a socialist and Marxist critique of traditional humanism.

The most influential thinkers on the conservative humanist side of the generation of '36 were Ortega, Heidegger and Zubiri. Tierno and Castilla, on the other hand, are indebted primarily to Anglo-American sociology and to Marxism.

Ortega y Gasset has left disciples in Spain and America. On the

Peninsula, Marías, Garagorri and Granell are the better known. Laín, although not quite a disciple, borrows two basic notions from Orteguian thought: the existential function of belief *(creencia)* and the idea of vocation as an authentic mode of being.

The influence of Heidegger on the postwar generation is extensive. There is hardly a work of philosophy that does not quote him generously. The poet L. F. Vivanco invokes Heidegger's definition of language for his *Introducción a la poesía española contemporánea;* Rof Carballo's entire critique of the psychoanalytic notion of human aggression is based on Heidegger's concept of thinking. For Laín, Heidegger is important because in a brillant and dramatic fashion he has put into question the empirical and rationalist method of inquiry.

A decisive influence on the liberal Catholics was the philosophy of Zubiri. Since Ortega's vital and historical reason did not provide these thinkers with a metaphysics or even an ontology, they looked to Zubiri's idea of *religación* (man's relation to the ground of all being) for a response to atheistic existentialism. Unfortunately, an excessive reverence for the person of Zubiri has left some of his disciples in an intellectual complacency they could ill aford. In the works of Marías, Laín, Garagorri, Rof Carballo and even the independent Aranguren one cannot find one critical statement on the philosophy of Zubiri, only routine praise. On the other hand, few men in European letters have shown a better understanding of contemporary philosophical issues than the heirs of Ortega and Zubiri.

Tierno Galván and Castilla del Pino have, under the influence of the social sciences, introduced a new critical sensibility into Spanish letters which is partly explored in this book. There is no doubt that their work will have a decisive impact on the concept of man and culture in contemporary Spain.

Since this study deals with representative Spanish thinkers, the reader may wish to know more about other essayists who have made significant contributions to the philosophy of culture. Some of these are Xavier Zubiri, Paulino Garagorri, Julián Marías, Manuel Granell, Francisco Fernández Santos, José Antonio Maravall, Domingo García Sabell, Gonzalo Fernández de la Mora, and Manuel Sacristán. It was my intention to confine this study to the Peninsular essay, and I have purposely chosen writers who have remained in Spain in order to better assess the direct interaction between expression and a particular socio-historical circumstance. A future study of this kind will deal with representative emigré essayists, such as Juan David García Bacca, Américo Castro, José Ferrater Mora and Francisco

Ayala.

A few final words are in order in regard to two points: first, as to the scholarly methodology of this book, and second about the audience for whom it is intended.

To my knowledge, this study is the first attempt in English to assess the importance of the Spanish essay after Ortega and the first critical introduction to the subject in any language. Since this is a pioneering work I have had to rely almost exclusively on primary sources for my evaluation of each writer. I should also mention the paucity of secondary works in this field and the fact that I have used them sparingly and selectively, distinguishing the few critical materials from adulatory reviews, trivial generalizations and mindless apologetics. A selected bibliography is included at the end of the study.

Of all the authors under consideration only Laín Entralgo has been the subject of dissertations and book-length studies;[19] the others, however, are widely and frequently discussed in every mayor literary journal and are even honored with *Festschriften,* but have not been until now the subjects of systematic analysis. The only broad treatment of mayor figures in the contemporary Spanish essay to date is Carpintero's *Cinco aventuras españolas,* a basically expository piece of work conceived around the unifying theme of "the problem of Spain."[20] With the exception of Laín and Aranguren, Carpintero and I have opted for different representative figures.

This study can be used profitably by graduate students and teachers of Spanish literature and culture, the historian and the instructor in philosophy (and the philosopher) unfamiliar with the Spanish language. It could prove particularly useful as a reference reader in a course in contemporary Spanish literature or history. I hope that these pages will inform as well as stimulate further discussion.

# Part One:

# Conservative Humanism

A generation is fashion: but there is more to history than costume and jargon. The people of an era must either carry the burden of change assigned to their time or die under its weight in the wilderness.

Harold Rosenberg, *The Tradition of the New*

# I. ESTHETICS AND POLITICS IN FALANGIST CULTURE (1935-1945)

In a commentary on the role of the artist during the Spanish Civil War, Carlos Mainer has described the dual style of Falangist literature as "on the one hand a classical austerity, both humanistic and counter-revolutionary, on the other, an inclination toward the destructive, the unconscious and the fantastic."[1] It is the purpose of this chapter to offer an analysis of the first type of literary expression with the aim of illustrating the interdependence of esthetics and politics in Falangist Spain. Kessel Schwartz, who has given us a good sampling of fascist attitudes toward Spanish literature and culture, confines his sources to the Seville-based Nationalist newspaper *ABC* (1936-39).[2] In this chapter I will trace the esthetic and intellectual roots of the Falangist view of culture to such elite publications as *Jerarquía* and *Escorial;* to the work of Eugenio d'Ors, the plays of Torrente Ballester and the essays of Laín Entralgo, Antonio Tovar and Eugenio Montes.

Walter Benjamin once remarked that fascism as he knew it offered people not their rights but an opportunity to express themselves. In contrast to communism, the objectives of which include the politization of the arts, fascism—observes Benjamin—introduced esthetics into politics.[3] The Nazi leadership's penchant for ritual, ceremony, pageant and spectacle is common knowledge; their aim was to conjure up the spirit of nationalism, nurture racial pride, instill a respect for tradition and create a mood for war. In its inability to deal directly and efficiently with social problems, fascism could not appeal to functional, pragmatic slogans; rather, its rhetoric sought to evoke images of a mythical, pathetic order emphasizing heroism, grandeur and destiny. The concept of revolution, more than a program of social transformation, had a strongly voluntaristic and esthetic meaning. Thus the poet Marinetti proclaimed war—often the objective of the fascist state—to be the most esthetic of experiences.[4]

In Falangist Spain, where imperial illusions and visions of a new Europe were linked to the performance of the Axis, the term esthetic seems especially appropriate, since the country's economic backwardness ruled out the possibility of successful military adventurism.

The Falangist movement—which José Antonio often called a "poetic politics," a "style of life," and "a way of being"[5]—had for its bard Giménez Caballero. As the editor of *La gaceta literaria* Giménez was very knowledgeable in all of the esthetic and political "isms" of the twenties and thirties and showed a marked enthusiasm for the totalitarian politics of Italy and Germany. Giménez, thoroughly versed in the poetic vanguardisms of his day, blended hysterical traditionalism, elitism, and revolution in a manner at first congenial to Falangism; but his association with the movement ran an erratic course and his religious fanaticism found more of a sympathetic ear among those who conceived of the war as a crusade than among the intellectual followers of José Antonio.[6]

An almost exclusive concern with the Spaniard's role in a national-syndicalist society persists in all the literary genres between 1936 and 1942, especially in the essay. Typical are the formulations of Falangist anthropology and philosophies of culture structured with images psychologically consonant with totalitarian dispositions such as hierarchy, order, unity, totality and discipline. The most predominant and significant imagery in the rhetoric of Falangism is that associated with geometry and architecture—both symbolic of the State. Publications of the day such as *Vértice* (1937-40), *Jerarquía* (1936-37), *Escorial* (1940-50) are obvious enough in the suggestiveness of their titles. A direct source of this esthetic inclination were the writings of Eugenio d'Ors, who inspired the short-lived but representative publication *Jerarquía*. Falangist intellectuals were particularly inspired by his *Las ideas y las formas,* a lengthy essay in which the Catalan philosopher attempted to correlate architectural forms with political institutions; these, he maintains, correspond to certain collective styles and historical rhythms. Also influential was Giménez Caballero's *Arte y Estado* (1935), a description of architecture's role as servant to the totalitarian state. To Giménez, architecture is the very essence of the state and Rome a model metropolis. The city, he writes, "is the point of balance between the individual and society," and great architecture, e.g. El Escorial, a "conquest of a mathematical formula of building."[7] Thus, in the first issue of *Jerarquía* the editorial heralds a new age of fascism whose strucutre and style would find its example in the geometric principles of classical architecture. The symmetrical (and thereby hierarchical) properties of classical models are to be the formal basis of a new social edifice, designed to convey the image of unity, totality, order and grandeur. Carrying the analogy further, the editor suggests class hierarchy when he notes that the outward lines of proportion, precision and beauty are but the manifest work of the anonymous but all-important artisan.[8] In the same issue Laín Entralgo speaks of giving direction, purpose and style to the fascist revolution through an architectonic structure of "the political genius of our age." Three years later, in the first issue of *Escorial,* Laín defines the monastery in terms of the new order: "religious in purpose, military in structure; serene, solid, balanced. . .like a State hewn from a rock."[9] Antonio Tovar also characterizes the revolutionary spirit as "a passion for geometry and a concern for all that is symmetrical and monumental."[10] García Serrano, in his first novel, *Eugenio,* envisages a society based on geometric principles, although his language is hardly one of reason and restraint. Recently, Albert Speer has revealed Hitler's obsessions with monuments and buildings as expressing the ideals of National-Socialism. The Führer's architect was commissioned to build the colossal geometric patterns of the great empires in history.[11]

For the Falange the esthetics of geometry were not confined to direct, overt political propaganda; they became the basis for a theory of culture and an image of man. The Orsian morphology of culture, specifically, the almost manichean opposition of two main styles, the Mediterranean (classical, Catholic, hierarchical) and the Nordic (Protestant, Romantic, liberal), became a rhetorical convention in the service of a totalitarian outlook.

A telling illustration of Orsian esthetics is Torrente Ballester's drama *El viaje del joven Tobías* (1938). This play, ostensibly an attack on psychoanalysis, is a philosophical dramatization of two opposing forces in human nature and society: the rational, spiritual and hierarchical against the irrational, demonic and anarchic. Torrente's purpose was to "convert artistic invention into pure geometry". . .by expressing lucidly the mystery of human destiny "in an effort at total rationalization."[12] The author explains the plot graphically by superimposing two triangles to illustrate a dialectical process by which the six principal characters interact in this scenic rationalization of human destiny. The upright triangle headed by the archangel Azarías represents the forces of sublimation and the domain of the spirit; the tip of the inverted triangle represents the diabolical forces of the unconscious symbolized by doctor Asmodeo. In Orsian terms the first triangle is classical, virile, angelic, and the second baroque, feminine, demonic.

The play centers around the unhappy Sarah, whose frigidity frustrates the consummation of nothing less than seven marriages. Following the classical Electra complex, she unconsciously identifies her successive husbands with her father. Asmodeo, symbol of man's libidinous nature and a caricature of Freud, labors assiduously, with the aid of devils, to arouse the passion of incest in both father and daughter. But Sarah finds salvation in the young Tobías, whom she was destined to meet through the divine intervention of the Archangel Azarías, who has assumed the guise of a wanderer. The young Tobías is introduced as a romantic, arrogant and undisciplined youth impervious to parental counsel and emotionally dependent on an indulgent mother. The archangel, while a guest in the Tobías household, subdues the young man's rebellious nature, strengthens the father's authority and finally puts an end to the tyranny of his perrenial rival Asmodeo. Sarah comes to know pure and genuine love and Tobías achieves self-identity and accepts parental and traditional authority.

The play is an adaptation of the book of Tobit from *The Apocrypha,* a combination of traditional Hebrew piety and Persian superstition. It is interesting to note that Torrente, at the height of a so-called "Catholic crusade," should resort to the strongly paternalistic and legalistic examples of Jewish morality and the spirit of the Old Testament and not to uniquely Christian sources. The choice becomes quite understandable when we discover that the Falangists had an obsession with father figures.[13] Just as the anonymous folklorist in the *Apocrypha* accepts a manichean view of the world, so Torrente opposes traditionalism and spirituality against modernism and the demonic. Yet considering the theme of the play and the intellectual climate in which it was written, it comes as somewhat of a surprise that the author should inject a good dose of humor and irony into his work.[14] After all, the subject matter is ultimately a theological problem, a conflict between God and Satan, structured along the neatly moralistic lines of an *auto sacramental.* But Torrente does not hesitate to make light of dogma or the messengers of God and frequently adopts an ironic attitude toward his major characters. This type of artistic self-assurance, intellectual boldness and moderate assimilation of the spirit of modernism is characteristic of the liberal Falangist temperament during the period of optimism, when the ideas of tradition, authority and personal destiny were still an essential component of a new nationalism and had not yet dissolved in bureaucracy, social fossilization and ultra-reactionary Catholicism.

It is perhaps Antonio Tovar who best reveals the pagan, modernist and distinctly secular-totalitarian strain in the Falangist ideology. Applying rationalistic principles to politics ("All the great leaders in history have built geometrically"), Tovar offers a singular interpretation of Sophocles' *Antigone* in which he makes a good case for the tyrant and questions the behaviour of the heroine. The protagonists represent the polar tendencies of political reality: Antigone is traditional, religious, irrational and reactionary; Creon is "revolutionary reason," irreligious, moralistic and modern. Tovar does not endorse unconditionally all of Creon's qualities and feels uneasy about the religious issue; but he circumvents it by cleverly undermining with a philological *coup de grâce* the authenticity of Antigone's religious beliefs and reducing them to superstition. The tyrant, on the other hand, wishes to destroy tradition with reason and replace the old religion of the Greeks with a new political morality. Unlike Antigone, whose individualism cannot inspire norms for general conduct, Creon imposes model behaviour for his citizens: "he exacts a type of conduct which is regular, clear and precise. . .What is important to Creon is a religion with rewards and punishments. . .a police-like religion."[15] Antigone is censured for "falta de sensibilidad para lo actual, lo político";[16] instead, she is concerned with the dead, the world of Hades and with egalitarian laws. For Tovar, Creon is the revolutionary tyrant who rationalized politics along geometric principles of order, clarity and precision for the common good; he is rational, virile and authoritarian. Antigone is the slave of a dark, blind, fantastic world; she is therefore not only and obviously feminine, but traditional, democratic and hysterical.

Such an essay could only have been written with full confidence in the triumph of European fascism. It is an interpretation Tovar would soon regret, since it poses a problem which after World War II became a topic among the liberal Falangists: the ethical component of politics. A number of events changed the ideological perspective of these idealistic social architects, among them the gradual exclusion of Falangist intellectuals from policy-making decisions in the Franco regime; on the European scene, the battle of Stalingrad; and finally, the defeat of the Axis, which created in Spain a cultural immobility and intellectual stupor where only a bland, vague and pedantic ethical critique of power and politics was possible.

As far as the rationalization of life and politics of Torrente and of Tovar is concerned, it seems fitting to define further the intellectual basis of their *Weltanschauung*. Both, while writing in the midst of a civil war that was proclaimed a religious crusade, actually downplay or ignore the dogmatic, ecclesiastic aspect of faith. They combat materialism, individualism and democracy, yet their so-called spiritual, hierarchical values, especially Tovar's, are those of a secular culture. For example, Tovar was contemptuous of religion, while Torrente was fascinated with psychoanalysis. The substance of what constitutes the Spanish essay from 1935 to the second Vatican Council (1962) is this ambiguity with respect to values, specifically the rationalist tradition.

Since 1942 this critique of reason on the part of the Falangists (Montes, Maravall, Laín) coincided with the historicist critique of Ortega, but in the context, of course, of a Catholic metaphysics. But from 1935-39 it was the Orsian concept of culture that prevailed, soon to be displaced by the authority of Heidegger and later Ortega, both more congenial than the Catalan esthetician to the followers of José Antonio. Thus, we must begin the Falangist critique of the secular tradition with d'Ors, who will give us a more precise meaning of the often-used terms "racionalización" and "espíritu de geometría".

Falangist rationalism was of a distinctly Platonic order, free of all Cartesian or Galilean implications. When d'Ors spoke of rationalism he meant esthetic reason proper to the forms; his militant idealism was inimical to all scientific, pragmatic or utilitarian rationalism characteristic of the secular age. Hostility to the Cartesian tradition, to the Enlightenment and to the technological revolution (instrumental reason) became one of the most persistent themes of the postwar essay. Reason as an essentially esthetic faculty is a favorite Orsian topic; here are two observations taken from his *Poussin y el Greco:*

> We call Ideas concepts when—directly, not allegorically—they can be sculpted. Here we find ourselves at quite a distance from intoxication: we are in the vicinity of Geometry. (Of Geometry, not of Analysis). . .
>
> Scientific progress as the growth of information is the result of curiosity, of an irrational, diabolical and *revolutionary* impetus. The demands of rationality on the other hand appear before scientific progress as a kind of conservative resistance.[17]

> Llamamos Ideas a los conceptos cuando—directa, no alegóricamente—pueden ser esculpidos. Aquí nos encontramos lo más lejos posible de la embriaguez: nos encontramos en la vecindad de la Geometría. (De la Geometría, no de Análisis). . .El progreso científico, como empresa de enriquecimiento de noticias, se lo debemos a la curiosidad, empuje irracional, diabólico, *revolucionario* siempre contra

la legalidad lógica constituida. En cambio, la exigencia de racionali-
dad representa, ante el progreso científico, una resistencia, por decirlo
así, conservadora.[17]

This type of "geometría sensible" or mathematical, rather than
applied reason, was the basis of a Falangist metaphysics, and a kind
of secular version of religious dogma consonant with authoritarian
politics. The principles of geometry, like those of Catholic theology
are dogmatic, i.e. axiom, theorem; yet they are the ultimate symbol
of the rational, universal order. Geometric reason reflects the spirit of
what d'Ors called Catholic, Mediterranean clarity, that is, a figural,
sensuous reason as opposed to the introspective, individualistic tem-
per of the North. Finally, the symmetrical lines of Geometry imply
hierarchy and a necessary and logical interrelationship of elements.
In short, geometry is symbolic of the rational, purposeful and orderly
structure of mind, spirit, nature, society (State); it is the quintessence
of pure form, and therefore the supreme expression of the esthetic,
contemplative, abstract-sensible world as opposed to the applied,
transformational reason proper of technology.

Thus hostility toward scientific rationalism also included a re-
jection of individualism and democracy, which were thought to be
the cause of dehumanization. Eugenio Montes, writing in *Escorial,*
decries the degeneration of reason into instrumentalism, the substi-
tution of materialism for spiritual values and the advent of the *homo
faber.*[18] Technology, argues Montes, has obliterated time and space
and converted man into a lost, fearful creature, unable to decipher
his destiny in an automated world. Torrente Ballester writes an *auto
sacramental, El casamiento engañoso,* in which Man is induced by
"Leviatán" (Capitalist State) and "Ciencia" to marry the latter's
daughter, "Técnica". This "deceitful marriage" gives birth to "Má-
quina", who eventually enslaves Man. The allegory develops as the
people ask "bread and circuses" of "Leviatán", who has exhausted
Man's will to produce under the relentless pressure of "Técnica" and
"Máquina". "Leviatán", unable to meet popular demands, asks the
help of the "Arquitectos" (Marxism) in a tacit agreement to recon-
struct the State at the expense of Man. The play concludes with the
rebellion of Man against all forms of repression in the name of per-
sonal freedom and his obligation to God. Torrente's *auto* is relatively
free from totalitarian apologetics; his principal target is materialistic
society embodied in both Capitalism and Marxist Socialism. In an-
other drama, *República Barataria,* an attack on communist revolu-
tionism as well as aristocratic indifference, Torrente singles out not

23

so much the revolutionary social aims of the Republican cause as the positivistic and to him, pseudo-scientific ideology which underlines a false theory of progress. The author castigates not the revolutionary activist, whom he takes seriously and treats with some understanding, but the intellectual, the architect of a scientific utopia, who is portrayed as a loquacious imbecile.[20]

But as critics of technology and scientific utopia, the Falangists are intellectually indebted more to Heidegger than d'Ors. The notion of "geometría sensible" was in vogue only during the Civil War, when it afforded an esthetic schema for a new Fascist State, although the concept was part of the Zeitgeist well into 1944. The most vociferous exponents of Orsian cultural categories were not the better known Falangists (Laín, Tovar, Maravall, E. Montes, S. Montero Díaz, etc.) who since 1936 felt closer to Ortega and Heidegger, but those disciples of the Catalan master who after the war would pass into obscurity. Of the liberals only Torrente shows a definite Orsian influence. In 1940, with both *Jerarquía* and *Vértice* defunct, the Falangists formed the more subdued cultural monthly, *Escorial.* Under the editorship of Laín and Ridruejo, *Escorial* signaled a partial break with the bellicose and fantastic rhetoric of the war years and the beginnings of a new intellectual posture. Aranguren has observed the transition with the following summary statement: "The moment has passed; history will not repeat itself. From now on Falangist thought will always preserve the influence of d'Ors, but confounded now with the philosophy of Ortega and Heidegger."[21]

Over the ten years of *Escorial,* only one article appears by d'Ors himself and two essays on his philosophy by Aranguren. The historicism of Heidegger and Ortega proved more substantial and profound than Orsian thought and served as an ideal weapon against Cartesian rationalism and technological dehumanization. Furthermore, Heidegger's mystique of being unto death, his concept of destiny and of ethical resolve were far more congenial to the romantic Falangist temperament than the superficial "angelología orsiana."[22]

In the pages of *Escorial* we still find an esthetic view of reality— esthetic in the sense that culture in general was more of a refuge than the result of the necessary tensions between artist and society. Many contributors, sublimating class interests, still dreamt of a Platonic society of heroic *hidalgos* amidst the ruin and misery of a nation devastated by civil strife. Yet many sensed that the myth of heroic Spain had come to an end and that their military success was a Pyrrhic victory. This sense of failure and guilt set in motion a concern for the ethical basis of the new regime.

For José Antonio, political action attained meaning and justification in the context of sound ethical principles. In 1941 Laín Entralgo, fearful that Falangism might be misinterpreted as a pagan, Machiavellian political program, wrote *Los valores morales del Nacional-sindicalismo.* In the same year López Ibor, who was not a Falangist but a traditionalist, wrote a petulant article on the "Pathos ético del hombre español" in which he says, among other things, "a Spanish woman knows more about ethics than the majority of the European masses."[23] But the shift to ethics actually stems from the political impotence of those who once set the guidelines for a social revolution and who now found their ideals betrayed by a cynical, bureaucratic regime that was beginning to exclude them from power. Since they could not criticize the status quo in political terms, their only recourse was to demand justice with the proper outrage, yet accepting the fact that the injustice was the political structure itself. In 1945 Javier Conde, with his *Teoría de las formas políticas,* shows the moral bankruptcy of modern totalitarianism and subordinates the political act to the ethical framework of civil law. In the same year Corts Grau, reviewing in *Escorial* one of the many treatises on the relationship between ethics and politics, avers that the relationship between the governor and the governed is essentially ethical and "la inmoralidad y la injusticia implican aberración axiológica".[24] As the euphemism "axiológica"—in place of "política"—implies, direct reference to existing conditions were carefully avoided; instead, a cryptic, obscurely elusive language abounded in all political studies. Thus, as fascist totalitarianism failed in Italy and Germany and as Franco codified a regime along the lines of the Counter-Reformation, the only dissent permitted in the arena of political controversy (academic controversy, of course) was that which could be couched in ethical language.

After the Axis defeat, theories of a united Catholic Europe inspired by the books of Christopher Dawson replaced the hopes of a new fascist millennium.[25] But within Spain the disillusionment and stoicism of those cut off from direct and effective participation in the affairs of their country takes the intellectual form of a hermeticism and an "intimismo" nourished by religious faith and accentuated by the impact of existentialism. As citizens, the authentic Falangists' social effectiveness was limited to ethical criticism of existing conditions; and this constituted their consciousness as intellectuals in Franco's Spain. Raúl Morodo has called this consciousness, which actually reflects a typical trait of the postwar essay, a "mala conciencia": "A false consciousness that appears in Spain from time to time and which is linked to a rationalized view of reality—to an 'ethical' view understood almost exclusively from an individualistic point of view."[26]

Here then, in summary, are the high points in the Spanish essay from 1935 to 1945. The Falangist intellectuals who became known through *Jerarquía, Vértice* and *Escorial* between 1935 and 1945 formed a view of culture under the initial influence of Eugenio d'Ors and after the Civil War under the more substantial and pervasive influence of Ortega and Heidegger, both constant although at first latent presences among the liberal Falangists.

Inasmuch as they criticized instrumental reason, the advent of the *homo faber,* and dehumanization through technology, the Falangists were no different from the majority of European intellectuals who reacted against the idea of progress; but their traditional and Catholic background forced them into an ambivalent and often hostile attitude toward the very irrationalist philosophy directly responsible for the destruction of the myth of progress. Against the fragmentation of esthetic unity by the modernists (Vanguardism, Joyce, Picasso, etc.) they projected the geometric, neoclassical formula of a new totalitarian culture. Instead of the prevailing trends of both artistic nihilism and liberal democratic institutions they put forth Ignatian discipline, hierarchy and paternalistic authority. To some extent the Falangists were very much like the English anti-democratic intelligentsia (Pound, Eliot, Yeats, Windham Lewis) who lamented the absence of heroic values and blamed democracy for the deterioration of cultural standards.[27] Perhaps men like Laín, Rosales and Ruiz-Giménez felt closest to the position of T.S. Eliot, who like Christopher Dawson—frequently quoted by Laín—felt the authenticity of Europe resides not in secular humanism but in spiritual, that is, Catholic, unity.

Yet, in spite of their obsession with balance, order and unity, the revolutionary impetus of the Falangists could not but absorb the romantic irrationalism of a Nietzschean will to power, which also accounts for the esthetic rather than ethical inspiration of their politics during the Civil War.[28] In this fantastic, unconscious and destructive facet of Falangist ideology one finds ludic, military, nautical, religious, and poetic language, complementary to the rhetoric of architecture and geometry. A study of the Nietzschean aspect of Falangist literature, however, is beyond the scope of the present chapter.

# II. LAÍN ENTRALGO AND THE TOPICS OF HUMANISM

## 1. Humanistic Discourse: Models, Examples and Formulas

The principal theme in the essays of Laín Entralgo is the notion of human perfection, conceived first as self-development through vocation and secondly as the oblation of truth to a transcendent, spiritual order of meaning.[1] Laín appropriates Ortega's definition of vocation as a unique personal process of authentic self-realization; a form of existence in which man is willing to risk his being in the pursuit of an ideal self.[2] Laín however, does not accept Ortega's historicism: man has not only a biography and a history, but also a nature or an essence which can either be degraded or enriched but never radically altered. Likewise, Laín believes that historical truth has a relative and not an absolute value, but he goes beyond historicism in affirming that historical truth, when it does not contradict Catholic dogma is a recapitulation of a revealed eternal truth and the enrichment of the Word. When historical truth assumes an absolute autonomy (i.e. secularization), it becomes for Laín an aberration, deformation, or deficiency of an eternal transcendent truth (e.g. Marxism).

Laín's rhetoric of humanism is the expression of two discernible motives in his work: absorption and subordination. The task of the humanist here is to absorb the import of historical knowledge and reconcile the secular with the religious and the temporal with the eternal, within a hierarchical unity. The most effective way of introducing the above mentioned themes is with a commentary of three key essays in which Laín examines the work of Picasso, Sartre and Michelangelo.

Laín's essay on Picasso (1964) introduces the neologism *prereligioso* which designates an aberrant or deficient form of religious experience. Picasso's work reflects for Laín an atheistic position of metaphysical and moral dimensions: metaphysical because of the artist's attempt to "capture all of reality;" moral because of his profound awareness of human suffering.[3] Ten years earlier Laín would not have conceded a pre-religious status to Picasso's work for at that time he could not divorce the idea of an atheistic consciousness from the notion of existential despair. In *La espera y la esperanza* (1955) for example, he affirms, echoing Zubiri, that without the recognition of God as the source and ground of all Being, man can only express his freedom in the form of radical despair.[4] Furthermore, atheism does not have an independent, autonomous standing, for it can only be arrived at through a negative relationship to God, by an inverse process of deification. In other words, for Laín atheism is impossible without God. In the Picasso essay Laín still believes that atheism is an aberration or deformation of theism but he has mollified his position and made some concessions to the unbeliever. Atheistic art and literature need not be *only* a defiant self-affirmation of existential despair but can be, as Picasso suggests, a sportive, ironic vision of life, a Sisyphus-like existence in which the artist can both protest against injustice and laugh at the futility of his efforts. The pre-religious attitude is a deficient encounter with the mystery of human existence and only a preamble to "truth," and like atheism it is a term the meaning of which is totally subordinated to Laín's categories.

If Picasso represents a deficient form of the religious experience, Sartre's notion of the absurd is for Laín an aberration of Belief. Just as for Heidegger anxiety is a primary disposition of *Dasein,* so for Laín belief *(creencia)* is an equally constant mode of being which constitutes an ontological structure of existence. In fact, Laín's anthropology of hope had its beginnings, in 1941, as a response and complement to Heideggerian thought. In *La espera y la esperanza* the author accepts Ortega's idea that belief is the ground of all our relations to the external world and enables us to take for granted a particular version of reality (e.g. culture). As such, belief is an existential precondition of planning and action.[5]

In the essay "Soledad y creencia" (Solitude and belief) Laín gives us a phenomenological analysis of belief, its relation to the control we have over our acts and its link to an understanding of ultimate reality.[6] He begins by pointing out the difficulty in defining the limits of the possessive pronoun mine *(lo mío),* observing that it cannot be apprehended through reason because self-knowledge understood as that which is my own (i.e., bodily functions) must be ultimately trusted, that is, believed in, in addition to being known. Next, Laín affirms that belief in a metaphysical sense can express itself in at least two forms: as refuge *(refugio)* and as daring *(osadía)*. Belief involves daring because man, "the animal of realities," always thirsts for more reality than is available to him; refuge, because it gives respite to man's search for ultimate reality and provides the assurance necessary for minimal security from doubt and anxiety. But refuge, claims Laín, should only be provisional, since progress in truth always requires daring.

At this point Laín introduces three possible attitudes in man's search for ultimate reality: the rationalist Hegelian, which holds that the historical unfolding of the rational spirit will eventually explain all reality; the Sartrian outlook that the thirst for ultimate reality is an unquenchable and futile passion; and Laín's own belief in a total satisfaction of man's search for a reality which is transcendental, transtemporal and supernatural and which guarantees an eternal mode of being *(ser para siempre)*. But now we are asked: "Doesn't the path of Hegel, Comte and Marx assume a fundamental belief that is all-inclusive *(abarcadora)* and everlasting *(para siempre)?*"[7] Laín does not recognize an independent, autonomous status to secular consciousness, but rather, subordinates it to his own categories by shifting the method of argumentation from demonstrative, dialectical proofs to ethical reasoning and *ad hominem* arguments. Here, for example, is an excerpt from his critique of Sartre's notion of the absurd:

> What Sartre calls "Absurd"—thus, with a capital A, to emphasize with a certain solemnity its invincible and unavoidable character, is only the name of a "great belief," that underlying and tacit "root belief" that allows him to give meaning to his work and to his daily acts of assent. Without the tacit support of each of those daily assents by a "great belief"—the fundamental belief "forever" in which they achieve ultimate meaning—life would be impossible.

> Lo que Sartre llama "Absurdo"—así con mayúscula, para patentizar con cierta solemnidad su carácter invencible, absoluto—es sólo el nombre de la "gran creencia", de la subyacente y tácita "creencia matriz" que le permite otorgar validez a sus obras y asentimientos de cada día. Sin el tácito apoyo de cada uno de los asentimientos cotidianos de una "gran creencia" soterraña—la creencia fundamental o "para siempre" en que todos ellos logran último sentido—no sería posible vivir.[8]

Now it is true that rationalist utopias as well as existential atheism are by philosophical definition beliefs; but surely the Sartrian notion of the absurd is not an "everlasting belief" *(para siempre)* in the way Laín's is. The difference is so radical that to refer to both attitudes as beliefs is to obscure the substance and uniqueness of the Sartrian concept. It is true that in everyday life one cannot but act upon beliefs which mediate between our consciousness and the external world; but the absurd is not so much an ontological datum as a philosophical doctrine, an acquired, provisional anchorage in the reality of values, soon to be replaced by another equally provisional "ultimate belief." The psychological disposition proper to this belief is the acceptance of contingency, a resolute decision to live in ambiguity and relativism. To insist, as Laín does, that contingency too is a belief is technically and formally correct, but it begs the question in the context of the uniqueness of Sartre's experience. By subordinating Sartre's experience of the absurd to his own categories, Laín formally invalidates a pristine, authentic, and autonomous expression of atheism.

In a sense the terms "pre-religious" and "belief," applied to Picasso and Sartre respectively, refer to the imperfect manifestations or shadows of an ultimate reality. All philosophical doctrines of course, have their own model of the real with its hierarchical terminology. But although Marxism, for example, also may have its ultimate and subordinate terms, it is primarily concerned with differentiating itself from what it considers its derived negative forms (superstructures) and with their negation. Laín, on the other hand wishes to establish a sense of kinship and common philosophical ground between two radically different views of life. His philosophical argument is weak, for it overlooks the uniqueness and autonomy of the "pre-religious" and "absurd" experiences; but these terms, even in the context of their subordination to ultimate order, serve a rhetorical function. Picasso and Sartre are not opposed; their views are not negated but rather seen as *participants* in a hierarchical spiritual order. The terms "pre-religious" and "absurd" are affective links to "the other" (*comprensión del otro*), gestures toward a common ground and an implicit plea for dialogue.

## The dignity of belief

The concept of belief carries a strong ethical connotation in the work of Laín and he employs the term to dramatize his role as a Catholic intellectual in the historical crisis of 1936. In the concluding chapters of *España como problema* (1949) Laín assesses the role of his generation in contemporary Spanish history. The essay "Los nietos del '98 y el problema de España" is essentially an *apología* for the Falangist view of the Civil War. In spite of its distinctly confessional and pathetic tone, the piece is a lucid evocation of the conflict of the early thirties and a vivid portrayal of the dilemmas of an upper middle class Catholic intellectual caught between two historical alternatives.

Laín presents his personal dilemma and the problem of Spain in 1936 in existential-ontological language: for the so called "grandsons of 1898" the historical crisis was a matter of "being or non-being;" the mood of the times is described as "historical anxiety" *(zozobra histórica)*—a deep anguish over personal and national destiny and the fear that a style of life, the very structure of daily existence, was doomed to disappear.[9] The ensuing tragedy and its political consequences, however, are for some Falangists little comfort, and Laín's often-quoted lament: "Mine is a bloody and spiritually splintered generation"[10] has marked this essay as a kind of characterization of the repentant Falangist consciousness.

Now Laín begins to justify his solidarity with the nationalists by posing the following question: How does one choose an historical destiny which is secure and certain and at the same time harmoniously linked to knowledge? To this he will answer that "destiny and knowledge cannot be harmoniously joined unless the beliefs by which the former is determined consist in *truly believing that the substance of that which is believed is the truth.*" In short, "there is no dignity without belief."[11] The option confronting the young Laín is not presented in political terms but in broad cultural categories, thus, "on the one hand the affirmation of national and Catholic values; on the other, the categorical negation of those two principles or the affirmation of those values which excluded them. Each one of us choose according to the dictates of his biography."[12]

The essay on the "grandsons of the generation of '98" reveals the principal motives of Laín's thought, placed here in the historical context which shaped them. His concern for the perennial problem of the essence of Spain finds here its frankest and most dramatic expression. Equally manifest is Laín's affirmation of faith by a Catholic intellectual in the contemporary world. The conceptual structure of the essay also reveals the existential framework of his anthropology—based on the notion of belief as an ontological structure of existence, fused here with Heideggerian and Orteguian ethics but subordinated to Christian metaphysics. Clearly, the confession or apologia is a reply to the challenge of secularization and its philosophical and ideological components: historicism, atheism, dialectical materialism. Against historicism Laín offers an intrahistory of Spain; against atheism and the notion of contingency—the dignity of belief.

## What is Humanism?

The enthusiasm and curiosity for the complexity and wonder that is man found its most dynamic expression in Renaissance literature and scholarship. In sixteenth century Europe the motto *Nihil humani a me alienum puto* characterized the proponents of a naturalistic world-view as well as those Christian philosophers who sought to support faith with the best of secular thought. Although Laín's humanism must be defined in the context of the twentieth century, his philosophical temperament reveals an affinity with the Renaissance spirit. The rhetorical *admiratio* of the grandeur of man, the cultivation of eloquence, a respect for tradition, the search for a synthesis of knowledge, the need to establish harmony between reason and faith, contempt for extremism and violence and a concern for the personal rather than a sociological ethic are intellectual traits common to men like Pico della Mirandola, Erasmus and Laín Entralgo.

How does Laín conceive his role as a humanist in the contemporary world? Invoking Saint Paul's metaphor of cosmic recapitulation in Christ and Aquinas' notion of *analogia entis* he dramatizes his function as a Catholic intellectual in the modern world within the framework of Christian eschatology. That is, Laín holds that when a Christian exercises his "will to historical fulfillment" *(voluntad de plenitud histórica)* the novelty of his intellectual achievement becomes a temporal, analogical replica of the absolute and infinite novelty of the word become flesh. The Christian in this sense is a microcosm in the giant macrocosm which is the history of humanity.[13] The implications of the concept of recapitulation for a Christian humanism are the idea of a past which, while being preserved, is continually regenerated both through historical novelty and the eschatological promise of the glory of the sons of God. We may interpret Laín's scheme to mean that the past contains the substance of the things to be hoped for, while the present provides a selective enrichment of the Word.

The analogical concept of recapitulation is a precise description of the aims of what has traditionally come to be known as humanism. In broad terms, humanism is a quest for values to be appropriated from the aggregate wisdom of the ages and the task of the humanist is to reproduce the best that has been written in the hope that it can impart an ethical example to the present. It is precisely this concern with culture as result rather than active, methodical and systematic inquiry that constitutes, according to Allen Tate, the philosophical fallacy of humanism. For Tate naturalistic humanism lacks a philosophical ground and is merely "an effort to imitate by rote the natural product of culture; it is a mechanical formula for the recovery of civilization."[14] Christian humanism escapes this type of criticism since its appropriation of certain aspects of secular knowledge is subordinated to established ultimate values which serve as a philosophical center of action. Still, even if Christianity does give humanism a temporal context it would otherwise lack, its rhetoric aims at convincing us of the continual return, regeneration and recapitulation of an essential knowledge both in its temporal and eternal dimension.

Laín has defined humanism as the intellectual pursuit of the problem: What is man? and the exercise of an intellectual discipline which reveals the relationship between knowledge and human existence.[15] This definition obviously suggests not only a proclivity to philosophical anthropology, but implies the need for metaphysics and ethics—the essential components of classical humanism. Thus in referring to his own discipline—medicine—Laín has written that "for the physician to be a *tekhnites*—or 'artist'—he must know what is the nature of illness, what is the patient in the context of his particular illness, what is man and what is the cure. He is ineluctably confronted with the problem of this multiple 'what' and its ultimate significance."[16]

Since humanism is a quest for value, the humanist is by definition a moralist: he scrupulously endeavors that knowledge be channeled in the service of man and preserve his essential dignity.[17] Medicine in this sense is not only the art of curing the patient as a physiological "case" but becomes a science which takes into account the nature of man, that is, his "person." Consequently, Laín's entire anthropology is an elaboration of a Christian personalist ethic which holds that human nature is superior to and transcends cosmic nature. "If by Nature we understand the 'Cosmos,'" notes Laín, "man, a natural or physical creature, is at the same time fundamentally a 'transnatural' or 'transphysical' entity; and this dimension of his being, which constitutes his ontological uniqueness, is the source of his psychological uniqueness, his moral responsability and his freedom. It is this dimension, finally, which reveals that man, in addition to being 'nature,' is a 'person.'"[18] In a doctor-patient relationship this implies

33

that the patient's illness is not only a physiological phenomenon measurable by diagnostic techniques; it is a biographical, human experience in which the attitude of the patient is decisive. In anthropological terms this would mean that human existence is an *a priori* datum, that is, anterior to any reductionist or abstract formulas based on empirical or rationalist presuppositions which arbitrarily choose to understand only a fragment of human reality.[19]

## The vocation of being human and the cardinal virtues

Laín's image of man centers on two ethical ideals, which when taken in the context of his Catholic anthropology of hope, form the foundations of his humanism: they are the idea of vocation and the ethics of courage and magnanimity. The first concept shows the decisive influence of Ortega and Heidegger; the second, while also important for Ortega, came to Laín through St. Thomas. "Vocation," writes the author, "is the path to authentic existence and our unique mode of being in the world. . . .Man is not only human by nature but also through his vocation."[20]

The essay that illustrates most dramatically the role of vocation in Laín's anthropology is "Michelangelo and the Human Body." In no other piece of writing does he express with more felicity his image of man than in his study of Renaissance genius. Laín isolates three conceptions of the human body in the sculpture of Michelangelo: the carnal, the personal and the spiritual. The substance of the essay is an amplification of the theme "body as person" exemplified by such models as "David," "Moses" and the "Pietà" of St. Peter's, which convey through gesture and bearing the distinct qualities of human dignity and grandeur. Laín's enthusiastic commentary on these statues becomes the rhetorical figures for his ethic of courage and magnanimity in the fulfillment of personal vocation and the acceptance of destiny.

Laín, who has always held that the body partakes even in the most spiritual of human activities, is impressed with Baudelaire's remark about Michelangelo's "Herculean Christ." In the essay, Hercules and Christ become the polar paradigms (flesh and spirit) that underlie, according to Laín, Michelangelo's artistic struggle to spiritualize the human body. It is a solitary and arduous struggle with which the author identifies.

In the statue of Bacchus Laín sees a reflection of the carnal body, the epiphany of man as mere nature. In the "Rebelling Slave" he

34

notes that "in his bearing and facial expression there is a strong evidence that this body is generating an intense desire for freedom."[21] But the fullest expression of the body as person is to be found in the statues of the "Pietà" of St. Peter's, "David" and "Moses," who are "yes-saying bodies to aspirations which the soul feels as a personal vocation." In the Virgin of the "Pietà," Laín notes that "the movement of her left arm, the expression on her face, what are they if not a bodily statement made by a person who freely accepts the tremendous burden of her vocation and destiny?" Of "David" he observes that "his body and gesture reveal to all a radical personal decision of a young man who is about to fulfill a mission of salvation."[22]

We have here the fullest expression of Laín's image of man: the courageous and magnanimous execution of an arduous task which defines his vocation and destiny. These virtues are the mark of the "great-souled man" of classical antiquity; for St. Thomas and Laín, they are also the ingredients of authentic Christian hope and the most effective antidotes to pusillanimity and despair.

Laín's view of man is consonant not only with that of St. Thomas Aquinas but also with an ethical creed exemplified by Nietzsche and Ortega: highly individualistic in its morality and edifying in its life style. Laín's encomium of Michelangelo's moral giants only reflects his own joyous dedication to personal perfection, a thirst to "be more" or what he calls "la empresa de ser hombre," the vocation of being a man.

The last section of the essay carries the subtitle of *"Acompañada soledad;"* here Laín wishes to accompany Michelangelo in his "permanent solitary struggle" to spiritualize the human body. Two observations are in order here. First, the idea of personal and spiritual genesis as a difficult solitary process is perhaps Laín's strongest affirmation of individuality. Yet it is a paradoxical solitude because the keener the solitude the more intense the presence (the company) of humanity *(cuanto más solo, menos solo, más amplia e intensamente acompañado")*. Another point of note is Laín's recourse to the art of sculpture as a figure of thought to communicate analogically the role of vocation in his image of man. Laín is a "sculptor of his being" as Ganivet—the most solitary of all modern Spanish essayists—put it in the the title of his only play, *El escultor de su alma.* Michelangelo's effort to shape the spiritual body corresponds to Laín's continuous struggle to "acquire more being" *(ser más hombre.)* Both personality and spirituality are here the inexhaustible sources of human growth; inexhaustible in meaning and as unfinished as the Pietà Rondanini.

In an essay on the art of reading and the quest for perfection Laín has written that "man, the sculptor of his existence, fulfills through reading the project he has before him,"[23] becoming in the process a more perfect person. The drama and incentive of human existence rests on the idea that "perfection always remains vulnerable and man considers himself always midway in his journey."[24] The process of spiritualization is arduous and unending, becoming more difficult as man demands more and more of himself in the fulfillment of his vocation and destiny. The paradigms of Hercules and Christ are the conceivable anthropomorphic limits of man as nature and spirit.

In the essays on Picasso and Sartre the implicit formula for humanistic discourse was the dialogue. A glance at these essays, or for that matter any essay, will reveal a plethora of interrogative sentences directed at the reader. This abuse of a common rhetorical device points to the importance the author attributes to dialogue and participation.

The essay on Michelangelo provides the model for the pursuit of a personal vocation. The image of man as *sculptor* of his being represents the idea of intellectual development or *self-edification*. By emphasizing the sheer size and imposing prescence of the statues *(colosal, soberano reposo, pasmoso),* Laín communicates man's importance in the cosmos and his personal and spiritual *grandeur*. The structure of the essay, based on the three stages of self-awareness and the arduous progression of self-creation, is highly dramatic. Essentially, Laín has turned his subject matter into a spectacle, an exuberant exclamation or *admiratio* of the "wonder that is man," so characteristic of Renaissance humanism.


## 2. Humanism and Politics


*Background: the experience of the Civil War*

In 1936, young, optimistic and fully dedicated to the Falangist cause, Laín had this to say about the role of the Catholic intellectual: "Our mission. . .is to live in danger, to move about that zone of natural truth which borders on error."[25] But in 1942, as theoretician of the *Movimiento,* the substance of his message is quite different. "The liberal Catholic," he writes, "has a dangerous propensity to form a group apart. . . .Under liberal influences the Catholic loses his mili-

tancy. . .his attitude becomes pious, esthetic and excessively toler-
ant."[26] What in the life of Laín accounts for this shift from a guarded
liberalism to a rigid, spartan conservatism, comparable in many ways
to the xenophobia of the Counter-Reformation?

The change in Laín's attitude may be traced to at least three
causes: the personal experience of the war, the weak, ambiguous po-
sition of the "liberal Falangists" in the postwar regime, and the deep-
ening anxiety of these intellectuals about the fate of a united Chris-
tian Europe. Of Laín's personal experience it will suffice to mention
that his brother was a Communist and that further political division
and alignment in his family had resulted in fatal consequences. Laín's
continued plea for dialogue and concord among Spaniards stems
partially from intimate knowledge of the terror of fratricidal war.
Subsequent justifications of the Nationalist cause surely account for
many contradictions found in the essays of those years.

Laín's position was complicated further by his role of theoreti-
cian of the *Partido único* at a time when it was becoming obvious
that Franco was willing to grant only nominal recognition to the
Falangist intellectuals, virtually barring them from any meaningful
political activity.[27] A man of unusually high intellectual caliber and
of a moderately liberal political disposition, Laín, as *Consejero de la
Nueva Falange,* found himself between the Scylla of political obli-
gation and the Charybdis of ethical protest, often supporting a cause
he no longer believed in. During the Civil War, when the New Spain
of José Antonio appeared as a possibility, Laín and his comrades
thought that their ethical principles could be integrated into a pro-
gram of National-Syndicalism, but as authentic Falange ideals began
to wither, Laín, in his disenchanment, fear, and confusion, could only
give frantic lip service to a morally bankrupt regime. Hence, his frag-
mented intellectual position, which has been perceptively defined by
Tierno Galván as intellectual schizophrenia. After the Civil War,
writes Tierno, many Spanish intellectuals found themselves embark-
ed on an ideological venture in which they didn't really believe. This
accounts for the fact that three years after the Nationalist victory, the
Falangist ideology was merely a political formality. The Falangists
did not generally accept total commitment *(compromiso total);*
rather, they displayed an attitude that is closer to existentialist re-
solve than to authentic political commitment, to wit: "Involvement
is something which carries one along but about which objective rea-
son and the psychological process are not in harmony."[28] The result
is ambiguity, reticence, and evasion, because commitment is only

halfhearted. "On the one hand a person is what censorship wants him to be; on the other, what he would like to be. In this schizoid atmosphere the intellectual finds himself in a sad and difficult situation because he cannot even question freely his own tragedy as an intellectual."[29] Thus, on the one hand Laín founded with D. Ridruejo the journal *Escorial*—the first serious and genuine attempt to relax the crusading zeal of the new regime—yet at the same time he engaged in hollow Falangist apologetics, anti-liberal harangues and diatribes against the spirit of secularization. Even his purely theoretical works are contaminated with propaganda. Working in a political vacuum, burdened with pedagogical responsibilities and fearful of the possible destruction of a "Christian Europe," Laín takes refuge (1944) in Catholicism—freeing himself from temporal contingencies—and in stoicism and friendship which now replace political activism.

With an impending allied victory, Laín became keenly aware that the all-consuming fear of the initial post-Civil War years was the ever-present prospect of a total failure of National-Syndicalism. In a letter to Emiliano Aguado, perhaps the most intimate and poignant the author has published to date, he confesses that the Falangist intellectuals had assumed a responsibility both unique and momentous, quite unlike the mission of the previous generations. For men like Menéndez Pelayo, for example, there was little risk involved in preaching to Spaniards about their patriotic duty; but for the Falangists, claims Laín, the new regime was a calling involving total risk, that is, the risk not only of death, but of failure.[30]

The fear of failure expressed itself particularly in Laín's attempt to establish some pedagogical guidelines for the new generation of University students. For how could a responsible educator repudiate the intellectual treasure of the liberal and heterodox tradition in Spanish letters just to accomodate the political exigencies of a regime bent on reintroducing the narrow, self-sufficient and spiritually homogeneous social order of the Counter-Reformation? One course of action would have been to succumb to the demands of the neotraditionalists, who were eager to extirpate all intellectual vestiges of an "anti-Spain" and create a culture from the ideas of Menéndez Pelayo and Maeztu. As a genuine humanist Laín could not opt for this solution, and when the ultraconservative elements in the regime began to wage a campaign to place Ortega's and Unamuno's works on the index of prohibited books, Laín immediately and unequivocally opposed and denounced the move. On the other hand, open recognition of the merits of the Republican intelligentsia was, although not inconsistent with José Antonio's and the authentic Falangists' view of culture, contrary to the politico-religious guidelines of the very regime Laín was serving in the capacity of educational supervisor.

No wonder, then, that Laín should refer to his fellow Falangists as a "bloody and spiritually splintered generation;" for, at least in intellectual and pedagogical matters, he feels that in spite of enormous pressures to obliterate the liberal Spanish heritage and close the doors to secular European thought, the Falangists refused to distort the intellectual history of modern Spain. Remembering the difficulty of the early post-Civil War years, Laín writes:

> Halfway through our intellectual formation circumstances had placed us in a position to teach those younger than ourselves. How could we do this? Pretending to be intellectual Adams, declaring ourselves—how easy—self-sufficient? This we could not permit ourselves as Spaniards and as men. . .To teach, to integrate, to learn—these have been for many years of burning uncertainty the daily tasks of a few Spaniards thirsty for perfection of their country. . .Some recompense has been given to us, the "grandsons of the generation of '98": the certainty that we have honestly resolved in our minds and with our conduct, the intellectual problem of Spain.[31]

The Spain that Laín has always envisaged is a culture in which Cajal and Juan Belmonte, Saint Ignatius and Unamuno, Saint Thomas and Ortega could and should coexist in harmony and friendship.

From the above we can infer that Laín's attitude is consonant with two tenets of traditional humanism: his pedagogical credo is simply a restatement of the "topos of exordium" in classical antiquity which holds that the possession of knowledge makes it a duty to impart it and that to hide or distort knowledge constitutes a grave sin. Also a distinctly humanist trait, reminiscent of Erasmus and Montaigne, is the effort at mediation and reconciliation. The humanist abhors conflict, especially when it is expressed in the form of political extremism, and Laín therefore censures both radical secularism and neotraditionalism in Spanish history. Repulsed by fanaticism but wary of innovation, Laín found the post-Civil War climate quite inhospitable to a humanistic politics in which men could trust in the efficacy of dialogue and rational persuasion, and in which ethics are not divorced from power. His enthusiasm for traditional values earned him the contempt and vituperation of the reactionary pressure groups who thought he was soft on liberalism. In the eyes of the emigrés he was and is respected for his sense of personal integrity, but is not beyond suspicion for his political ambiguity; for, like his predecessor Menéndez Pelayo, Laín has been temperamentally unable to accept some of the inevitable philosophical implications of a new historical era.

## The Topics of Humanism

Our analysis of Laín's attitude toward secular values has revealed that when belief is affirmed authentically it bespeaks of the essential dignity of man because it forms the ground for self-knowledge, vocation and destiny. We have also seen in the author's critique of Sartre that belief as a basic structure of existence can serve as an affective link among men of different philosophical outlooks by revealing their common needs and aspirations. Laín strengthens and expands this bond rooted in the notion of belief by giving a contemporary cast to some of the topics of traditional humanism. For example, a leitmotif in his essays is the idea of friendship, a subject treated extensively by Aristotle, Cicero, Seneca and Montaigne. Now, to extol the virtues of friendship and make it, as Laín does, the ethical core of coexistence, may seem anomalous in an age of collectivism and group consciousness; but this emphasis on a limited, personal, and highly individualistic type of social commitment betrays in Laín not only a definite affiliation to classical humanism, but also a profound disenchantment with institutional forms of human solidarity. After the failure of José Antonio's highly idealistic form of fascism, Laín withdrew from politics and dedicated all his energies to writing and teaching. Among the Falangists a comradeship bound to a so-called unique historical destiny became depoliticized to remain a lasting friendship among a handful of intellectuals. Dignity and a personal style took priority over ideology; "the vocation of friendship" replaced the militancy for a new social order.

Laín's first collection of essays is subtitled "Ensayos de crítica y amistad" (1948); each essay is dedicated to a friend. Friendship constitutes for the author an integral function of intellectual pursuit: "Without an adequate dedication to the life of the intellect and without the cultivation of friendship in freedom," he writes, "I feel that I am not I and that I cannot be myself."[32] In his theoretical writings he has emphasized the role of friendship as the essential and structural prerequisite of all social behavior, whether it involves the doctor-patient relationship or the interaction between governor and citizen. As a philosopher and dramatist he has challenged Sartre's thesis that "Hell is other people" with his play *Entre nosotros,* which I will now examine.

## A Reply to Huis Clos

*Entre nosotros* lacks the dramatic power and artistic skill of Sartre's penetrating but limited view of interpersonal relationship, but it compensates in part for its bland and conventional treatment of human nature by offering a plausible corrective to the fatal opposition between subject and object of early Sartrian metaphysics.

The play is a dramatization of the problem of coexistence among a group of five archeologists on an expedition in the Egyptian desert. The initial scenes show four men and one woman busily at work in a spirit of teamwork and camaraderie. The leader of the group, Sir Philip, and Diana, his assistant, are lovers. A letter from London informs Sir Philip that the discovery of a theft perpetrated in the British Museum has implicated Diana. Sir Philip reads the letter to his colleagues, omitting the name of his mistress for reasons which are eventually revealed as an incapacity for confidence, openness and intimacy.

When Sir Phillip refuses to disclose the identity of the guilty party, mutual suspicion, mistrust and acrimony grow to an intolerable level and threaten the group's very coexistence. Sir Phillip can only think of the successful completion of the project, and therefore expects Diana to bear the burden of guilt alone; he also discourages any personal involvement on the part of others by appealing to their sense of decorum. Diana is subservient to Sir Phillip's aristocratic ethic in that she would rather endure the "hell" of others than unburden herself. Just as in Sartre's play the characters are deprived of their selves and are at the mercy of others who constitute their hellish existence, so Diana's self is only what others have made her: an object of mistrust.

One day, in the absence of Sir Phillip, Diana confesses her complicity in the theft and succeeds in establishing a truly personal (subject to subject) relationship with her co-workers. In the course of discussion they recognize that they were all mere instruments of Sir Phillip's narrow ethic of dignity and the means of his professional ambitions, for he had mistaken camaraderie for friendship and valued people not for what they were but for what they could do as a group. Camaraderie is the joining of two or more people for a common objective; friendship is a form of communication based on love, in which two people mutually perfect one another as human beings.

Laín concludes here that man is a constant possibility for the other to be either "heaven" or "hell." A master-slave relationship need not mark every human encounter, as Sartre would have it. There are authentic and inauthentic forms of *we:* when people are objects or instruments for others, or are subordinated to impersonal ends, the latter notion of *we* prevails; when human beings recognize each other as subjects endowed with freedom, a notion of self, and a psychological uniqueness, they are in a position to engender a genuine form of *we* whose basis is friendship.[33]

*Laín and Camus*

A more successful play of Laín's on the theme of coexistence, this time with political implications, is *Cuando se espera,* best translated as *The Waiting Room,* which offers many ideological parallels to Camus' *Les Justes.* Like the author of *L'Homme révolté,* Laín believes that all political acts must be accompanied by moral responsibility regardless of the injustice they claim to abolish, and that a revolution which ignores the moral imperative to respect the dignity and innocence of human life loses its legitimacy.[34] In short, if man is to retain his humanity as a political animal he cannot divorce ethics from politics.

In *Cuando se espera* Pablo, a theoretician in a triumphant socialist revolution, envisages for his country a social order in which the new regime, having eradicated the injustices of the old order, can make peace with the past and incorporate its cultural contributions. Symbolic of the old and defeated regime is Pablo's long time friend Martha, who is eager to leave the country at the first opportunity lest she fall victim to political reprisals. For Pablo it is both of personal and symbolic importance that Martha be permitted to leave in safety.

The entire drama takes place in the waiting room of the railroad station where Martha awaits her destiny and Pablo will test the moral mettle of his revolutionary ideals. As Pablo and Martha are waiting for the train a group of vindictive members of the revolutionary government have trumped up charges of treason against Martha and have instructed two guards to execute her as an enemy of the State. Pablo is helpless against this morally devastating verdict since he cannot countermand the orders of a superior officer; besides, he also is now implicated in the charges of counter-revolutionary activities. Martha is summarily executed and Pablo's utopia is blemished with the blood of an innocent human being.

Not only did Martha's death signal the revolutionary government's refusal to make peace with the past, but it also made manifest that when political ends are overzealously pursued human beings are often perceived not as persons but exclusively in terms of their social category. Even if Martha no longer professes the political views of her class and repudiates the old order, she is still forced to accept that past as her destiny and this is why she refuses to go into hiding. "Your comrades," she says to Pablo, "will not allow me to bury the corpse of the woman I once was. With their decision to arrest me they have turned loose my past upon me and now I cannot possibly repudiate it. . . .When in my deepest self I feel alien to that woman you know as Martha de Leoben, it is precisely then that I must affirm that woman with my conduct."[35]

But the central thesis of the play is the condemnation of political violence, even in the pursuit of just and human goals. What links Laín's views with those of Camus and the classical moralists is that he believes that there is a universal structure of values such as honor, dignity and innocence that cannot be set aside to acommodate far-off ideals and utopias. In Camus' *Les Justes* the following exchange occurs between Stepan, the cold, hardheaded revolutionary fanatic, and Kaliayev, who speaks for Camus' humanistic position:

> *Stepan*
> Innocence? I know what it is perhaps. But I have chosen to ignore it and to make it unknown by thousands of men so that some day it can take on a larger meaning.
> *Kaliayev*
> One has to be very sure that that day will arrive to be able to deny everything that makes a man want to live.
> *Stepan*
> I am sure of it.
> *Kaliayev*
> You cannot be. In order to know which of us is right it would be necessary to sacrifice perhaps three generations, to have several wars and terrible revolutions. When this rain of blood will dry on the earth you and I will have been long mixed with dust.
> *Stepan*
> Then others will come and I will greet them as my brothers.
> *Kaliayev*
> Others. . .Yes! But I like those who are living today on the same earth as I and it is they whom I greet. It is for them that I struggle and that I consent to die. And for a faraway city of which I cannot be sure, I will not strike the face of my brothers. I will not add a dead justice to a living injustice.[36]

Camus' moral sensitivity to violence and terror in the name of a "faraway city" is echoed in Pablo's final speech to his comrades:

> We are not the first, we are not the only ones, nor will we be the last in spilling innocent blood. But you and I have made a religion of human dignity. I have never been tempted by sentimentality; I believed always that struggle, with all its possible hardships and violence can be necessary for the triumph of a just cause. I say struggle, combat, not murder, which is often disguised as lawful action or political imperative. . .
>
> You have alluded, Helen, to "the cunning of reason:" words of an ideologue who wanted to save his optimism or his philosophical pride with a clever verbal pirouette. Before an imagined injustice, how easy it is to conceive that reason will ultimately absorb it and justify it! But when murder is a reality and a palpable fact, when we have heard the shot that caused it, the cunning of reason cannot make it disappear . . . .No, Helen, no; history can never justify murder. It can cover it up, make you forget it, but it can never justify it. Human life, any human life, has absolute value. Any and all human life.[37]

No doubt Laín is authorized to speak of the degradation of political ideals by violence, having experienced the evils of fratricidal war in his own country. He is also aware, as Camus was, that revolutions in our century have often resorted to unmitigated violence and have forcibly established totalitarian regimes. Denunciation of communist terrorism in the name of democratic individualism of course cost Camus his friendship with Sartre, for whom the socialist experiment was undergoing a difficult and even unpleasant stage, but a necessary stage nevertheless if bourgeois humanism were to be destroyed. Laín, like Camus, takes his stand with bourgeois humanism, opposing both the use of limitless terror in the name of injustice and the need of repression in the name of the future. Both men subordinate politics to the absolute value of human life.

*Leisure*

Another humanist theme fully exploited by Laín is the notion of leisure *(ocio),* the option to lead a life of contemplation directed toward personal perfection rather than submit to the slavish execution of professional or exclusively useful duties. As an intellectual attitude it implies a preference of speculation and understanding over ability and know-how, of metaphysics over pragmatism, in short, of theory over praxis. Laín, however, does not invoke leisure in name of privilege, nor does he mean to segregate dignified occupation from servile work. He utilizes the concept to impugn the values of a society obsessed with professionalism and specialization in which the routine and ritual of work is divorced from truly human potentiality; a society whose scientific community has permitted the total fragmentation and atomization of knowledge. According to Laín, leisure should serve first a therapeutic function as a corrective to the excessively practical and utilitarian orientation of science, which to the author constitutes one of the main causes of modern anxiety. Secondly, the spirit of *ocio* is an invitation to the specialist to widen his intellectual horizons with human letters. Finally, a relaxation of the purely pragmatic canons of the modern scientific outlook would facilitate the intercommunication and integration of today's diversified knowledge.

Laín invokes the classical notion of leisure which he describes as a state of being: "a non-utilitarian activity in which the soul acquires an exclusive and exemplary nobility."[38] The lack of leisure and the absence of the spirit of festivity in the contemporary world constitute what he calls "the sickness of the West." Men of all cities are slaves of "the religion of labor" and have substituted the classical notion of leisure for mere diversion. An authentic spirit of festivity would lift the anxieties created by values totally subservient to the marketplace. Festivity and leisure are interdependent dispositions since they both have a liberating effect and enable man to broaden and enrich the spirit. The *fiesta* is not an occasion for rest, nor the celebration of a memorable event: to celebrate an authentic holiday is "to leave behind everything which in our existence is historical, that is, the care *(cuidado)* for existence. . . .The *fiesta* returns to man the pure joy of an existence which thirsts for eternity."[39] Leisure and festivity, then, would be for Laín the ideal therapy for the existential anxiety inherent in a technological world.

# 3. The Rhetoric of Conservative Humanism

I have referred to Laín as a traditional humanist because his essays and dramas express values usually associated with permanence rather than change; his choice of topics reflects a preference for the fixed, the stable and the lasting: essence over accident and mutability, the eternal over the temporal. Now before I discuss Laín's conservatism it should be noted that I do not wish to apply any definition too strictly; the labels "conservative" or "traditional" would lose their meaning if used to categorize the author's views on the doctor-patient relationship, which show far more innovation than tradition. However, Laín's work by and large is that of a preserver of the best that Western thought has to offer; he is a brilliant exegete and teacher rather than an original thinker.

The question before us now is what can be properly called the rhetoric of traditional or conservative humanism; or, how do Laín's concepts, topics, and rhetorical modes and figures reflect the traditional humanist temper? I will attempt to answer this question by making a number of points.

The importance Laín attaches to the *concrete* person is a good case in point for traditional humanism. Laín, like Unamuno, frequently speaks of the concrete man, the individual as opposed to an abstract, depersonalized notion of man. Now it is true that traditional humanism has often been characterized by its predilection for abstract thought, the contemplation of inmutable truth, and the intellectual's ability to transcend and even deprecate the concrete. Although this may be an important feature of humanism, especially of the Platonic tradition, it is not pervasive. On the contrary, we know that Aristotelian and Thomistic metaphysics have a distinctive empirical orientation. Furthermore, as startling as it may seem, concrete values have a more compelling appeal to a conservative disposition than do abstract values. Chaim Perelman is correct when he observes that

> The need for reliance on abstract values is perhaps essentially connected with change. They seemingly manifest a revolutionary spirit. . . .Abstract values can readily be used for criticism, because they are no respecters of persons and seem to provide a criterion for one wishing to change the established order. On the other hand, where change is not wanted, there is no reason to raise incompatibilities. Now concrete values can always be harmonized. . .[40]

In spite of its cautious and tentative wording, Perelman's observation is precise and appropiate regarding Laín's humanistic values. The virtues of courage, magnanimity and the exercise of friendship are exemplary concrete values; and the message of *Entre nosotros* is surely the idea that the concrete individual has more value than a humanitarian ideal. Man does have a nature which constitutes his dignity; herein resides his concrete value as a man. This nature can be enriched, modified, but not radically altered, perverted, or subordinated to notions or uses extrinsic to his essential dignity. This is why the humanist in the traditional sense would not urge man to change, but rather to develop fully what is latent in him.

Now belief, by granting authenticity to man's vocation, is not only for Laín a form of assent that bestows dignity, but also comes across as a rhetorical figure asserting the need for permanence amidst change in man's personal life and in history. Through belief man can define his self and sanction his being in the world. Likewise, on the collective level to believe is to adhere to and identify with that aspect of history or "intrahistory" which remains impervious to change. Belief, in sum, is a rhetorical value for permanence, for the need man feels to preserve values, to rest in a particular truth and to identify himself truly with it.

There is another form of interaction between rhetoric and belief which brings into play the two kinds of argumentation discussed earlier—dialectic, which appeals to reason, and rhetoric, which appeals to belief. Let me reiterate here that for Laín self-knowledge, knowledge of the other, and man's relationship to God are ultimately grounded in belief. The function of rhetoric in this context is to order and rationalize those human potentialities which are not accessible to reason (dialectic) and belong to the realm of the irrational (that is, to belief), yet are vital to existence because they are the source of values. Friendship and hope, for example, would be eminently proper qualities worthy of development through rhetoric. A language that addresses itself to the human propensity for belief and directs it toward the good and the beautiful is the rhetoric of humanism. For Plato this was the language of myth and *ēpode* (charm, spell), a form of discourse capable of engendering new beliefs and strengthening old ones by virtue of its charm and beauty. The function of *epode* is pedagogical and psychological; it harmonizes the irrational part of the soul by releasing and ordering man's demonic powers, thus placing him in mutual relationship with the gods, and by inducing the soul to temperance and harmony (*sophrosyne*). For Laín, as for Plato and Aristotle, the ultimate end of rhetoric is ethical, that is, it is the means of inducement to accept values which are synonymous with happiness. The path to happiness is the practice of virtue, and the cultivation of friendship, for example, is an exercise in virtue, and therefore good and noble. The manner and form in which Laín urges us to practice some of these virtues which are the topics or *loci* of classical humanism will attest to his conservatism.

*Friendship and politics*

I have already made reference to Laín's disillusionment with politics after the Civil War and to his substitution of friendship for political commitment. Indeed, to exalt friendship is to endorse a form of interpersonal relationship confined to an individualistic and personalistic ethic, since it is based on equality and openness. It is precisely for this reason that Santayana has described friendship as a "distinctly selective, personal and exclusive form of relationship with a dignity utterly absent in the modern State."[41] Collective consciousness does to an extent submerge or sacrifice personal interest, mutual affection, and responsibility between two people to a common and general good; and in totalitarian societies the absence of trust most surely undermines the practice of friendship. A tyrant, a dictator, or a party apparatus are inhuman because they treat people as instruments, not as friends.

The eloquent language of *Entre nosotros* establishes the antithetical concepts of *person-instrument* and *friendship-camaraderie*. The concepts in the last dyad, of course, are ethically compatible provided that camaraderie is grounded in friendship, for otherwise it remains a mode of man as instrument. As one of the characters says of Sir Philip, "as so many people in our time, he had taken for friendship that which was mere camaraderie." To which his companion adds, "What could we do with a man who had reduced us to a condition of mere instruments. Instruments of his desire to complete as soon as possible this archeological expedition. Instruments of his personal view of human dignity."[42] It would not be difficult to see in these remarks a comment on the impersonality and degradation often inherent in politics when they are devoid of ethics. "Camaraderie" has in our time strong political connotations: unlike friendship, which is based on reciprocity, on autonomous and spontaneous cooperation bound to personal, individualistic ethics, camaraderie (political solidarity) is cooperation based on values often extrinsic to friendship.

The fact that the characters of *Entre nosotros* are archeologists is also significant because what they discover is a manuscript, twenty-four centuries old, which gives moral authority and universality to the values that the characters have discovered. The ancient scroll contains a dramatic poem very much in the tradition of the book of Job, recording the lamentations of the just sufferer. In this particular poem the sufferer understands his misfortune by opening himself to the pain of others. Again, the values which engender meaningful appreciation of "the other" and constitute the spiritual core of coexistence are the eternal values which each individual must discover for himself.

Laín's apoliticism, his suspicion of ideology, are founded on the bitter lessons of contemporary history in which moral monstrosities have carried "political" sanctions. The exercise of power without the guiding principle of value is tantamount to barbarism and therefore abhorrent to civilized men; and to the humanist in particular, man, as Erasmus held, must behave with decorum "in a manner worthy of his nature." If politics cannot justify this manner of behavior it is not a humanistic politics. In other words, politics is a means to human ends and those who will use it must be made aware of its ethical foundation. Laín feels that friendship is the basis for a possible politics because it is a truly human form of interpersonal relationship. In the meantime, politics is only a form of alienation for which he feels no vocation, lest he falsify his beliefs; as an intellectual he limits himself to an ethical revulsion of an unjust status quo. This ethical protest which avoids action manifests itself not as revolutionary rhetoric bent on change but as a plea for *compatibility*. Thus he aspires for a society in which "politicians, intellectuals, the military, public servants and workers would understand each other dialectically, each group through its own occupation."[43] The intellectual can discharge his civic responsibility as an intellectual, not as a politician. He may criticize only as a moralist, not as an ideologue.

The traditional humanist's distaste for politics, his scruples as a moralist, are at odds with the new notion of "humanitarian humanism" which will be discussed in another chapter. For while injustice, misery and exploitation do exist, the conservative humanist remains a man of patience who eschews direct political action for fear that, as Sartre said, he will "dirty his hands." He conceives of humanization as a slow, painful process of education and not a radical, precipitous change which only substitutes one form of oppression for another. The lesson of history for Camus and Laín (although the former's metaphysical revolt excludes him from the category of conservative) is that civilization is fragile and must be sustained even at the risk of prolonging its imperfections. A criticism could be levelled, however, against traditional humanism that while it affirms the concrete individual it does so, paradoxically, abstractly, by neglecting to consider man as an actor and sufferer in the *concreteness of history*. But this theme is the subject of another chapter.

## Conclusion: Laín and Teilhard de Chardin

Finally, a few words about Laín as a theologian in view of the fact that *La espera y la esperanza* is an ambitious and significant statement on the future of the cosmos within the framework of Christian eschatology. In this work Laín has developed a theory of hope based on the concept of human expectation as an ontological structure of existence and his views invite comparison with Teilhard's *The Phenomenon of Man.*

Laín is an outstanding philosopher and an exceptional man of science who has been unwilling to accept some of the implications and demands of a scientific age. An excessive caution and reticence in the use of religious language, and a predilection for apologetics of a world view that has collapsed, account for his failure to respond with sufficient intellectual vigor to the cultural imperatives of our time.

At a time when Teilhard had already broken down the metaphysical barriers separating Catholic philosophy from science, Laín was fearful of the "three grave wounds the Church had suffered since the Renaissance: the Reformation, Secularization and Modernism;"[44] and instead of incorporating, like Teilhard, the totality, the fullness of secular reality into his philosophy as the essential precondition of a new religious consciousness, Laín warns the Catholic thinker of the dangers of a non-spiritual involvement and operation in the world. The Spanish philosopher is also confident that secular values are on the verge of a breakdown, which again will occasion a turn to God and spiritual values.[45]

I do not wish to confuse here Laín's criticism of the evils of technology with his uneasiness in a secular age. To the former he has reacted in clear humanistic fashion by attempting to restore the prestige of metaphysics and insure a unitary view of knowledge. I only wish to single out a number of concepts in Laín's theory of hope which I feel are inadequate and cannot satisfy the demands of a new Catholic humanism, because they do not respond with sufficient force to the spiritual needs of a truly secular age.

One such concept is "methaphysical hiatus," used by Laín to remind the Catholic intellectual of "the abysmal difference" between scientific theory and dogmatic truth; that is, between a metaphysics postulated on the basis of human knowledge, and the metaphysics required by religious dogma.[46] Laín, however, narrows the gap somewhat between human and divine knowledge implicit in the concept by recourse to St. Paul's metaphor of the "impatient expectation:" *omnis creatura ingemiscit et parturit usque adhuc* (Rom. 8:19-22), which is given a metaphysical significance. The *gemitus creaturae* designates the radical ontological deficiency of creation which impatiently anticipates deliverance from servitude and corruption through the eventual appearance of the sons of God. In line with the subordination of categories, creation is generously given to man, who with the aid of reason humanizes the cosmos and directs it toward its divine purpose. The theological import of this notion is further interpreted and supported on the basis of a philosophical assumption which considers reality not as something static but views it as having a general tendency toward self-fulfillment; being in this sense is an active and primary operation, by virtue of which, things are not so much realities but operational nuclei of a reality that is coming into being. Consequently, the *gemitus creaturae* and the impatient expectation become evidence of the metaphysical structure of the real world awaiting redemption and fulfillment in "the freedom of the glory" which is the recapitulation of all the creatures in Christ. In this context, man with the aid of science participates in the redemption of the cosmos.[47]

From a historical perspective a term like "metaphysical hiatus" conveys a pre-Teilhardian world view. After *The Phenomenon of Man* it would seem foolhardy for a serious Catholic theologian to reintroduce the traditional divisions of God-World and Spirit-Nature and maintain the chasm between human and divine knowledge. Once the Spirit is understood to form part of the cosmos, science can in no way be considered apart from the general evolution and hominization (deification) of the universe. Science, then, is not a subordinate, oblative activity of man to a transcendent being, but is a process by which the immanent activity of Spirit (God) generates the eschatological movement until God and nature become fully one. The evolution of the cosmos, attracted by the Omega-point, is sustained by a transcendence, which, because it is also immanence, cannot alienate man either from nature or God. The distinction between divine and human (scientific) knowledge becomes anachronistic.

For Teilhard science is no myth, nor did he ever anticipate, like Laín, the collapse of secular values; rather in dialectical fashion he affirmed them denying their ultimate value. Human intelligence, believed Teilhard, is able to achieve "supreme consummation."[48] And supreme consciousness is not a link with a transcendental power but the "illuminating involution of being upon itself."[49] Finally, the eschatological consummation does not rest in a sovereign power that grounds our existence but in "the wholesale internal introversion upon itself of the noosphere;"[50] maximum consciousness, not salvation and celestial eternity, then, is the ultimate purpose of creation.

51

Laín's metaphysical notion of the *gemitus creaturae,* on the other hand, is historically a meaningful theological statement and is superficially consonant with Teilhard's evolutionary theories. But because Laín has even a broader scientific formation than Teilhard it is curious that he should neglect to formulate some of the scientific implications and dynamics of the Pauline metaphor. Laín's notion is deficient in that the so-called "servitude and corruption of the world" (its ontological indigence) is not placed with sufficient confidence under the power of science. Whereas the traditional Thomist distinction of *virtus propia* and *virtus aliena* is absorbed in Teilhard by the power of potential consciousness, Laín still identifies radical affirmation of scientific knowledge with Promethean arrogance.

The *gemitus creaturae,* then, would seem to include the Teilhardian notion of substance as process, but Laín's reluctance to welcome unequivocally the reality of the secular era and to endorse the redeeming function of self-affirmation through science, and his insistence on maintaining the dualistic functions of time-eternity, nature-grace, leave the Pauline metaphor with an aesthetic rather than a truly timely metaphysical meaning.

A consequent religious humanism must respond more energetically to our cultural imperatives than the theological language of Laín. As the distinguished Catholic philosopher James Collins has noted, the approach of an open religious humanism in our time should be "to search out the roots of the religious attitude in man's own structure and experience, as involved in active relationship with the physically and historically evolving universe."[51] Laín has searched out with significant success the religious attitude in man's structure and experience, but perhaps this anthropology is insufficiently grounded in historical reality. That our historical experience, in its most radical mundaneity, can be a rich source of religious consciousness has been ably demonstrated by Teilhard. Laín spuriously spiritualizes history without incorporating its mediating value. One can admire his aspiration for the eternal; yet our sympathies are tempered when we see that much of its impetus is derived from a need for security and immunity from secularization. One finds in Laín genuine hope which, if warranted from his personal point of view, is historically inopportune. For Laín is both behind and ahead of history; he is a man of memory and hope, the last spiritual offspring of the Generation of 1898.

# III. PSYCHOANALYSIS AND CULTURE: CREATIVE MYTHOLOGY IN THE WORKS OF JUAN ROF CARBALLO

## *Freud in Spain: An Outline*

When Ortega introduced German philosophy to Spain early in the century he did not neglect psychoanalysis, but it is well known that he was more interested in the incipient discipline of phenomenology as expounded by Husserl and Scheler than in the theories of Freud. Spanish intellectuals, like most of their European counterparts, did not take psychoanalysis seriously, and Ortega's extensive and sympathetic article on the subject written in 1911 remained perhaps the most responsible Spanish treatment of Freud for the next thirty-five years.[1] Yet, curiously enough, the first translation in Europe of the complete works of Freud appeared in Spanish in 1922. Psychoanalysis was received most favorably in the Anglo-American world while on the continent it was stubbornly resisted or ignored. It is difficult to measure the relative success of psychoanalysis, and we cannot discuss here the vicissitudes of the discipline in each country. Surely, Freud was familiar to artistic and academic circles in all of Europe since the success of *The Interpretation of Dreams* (1900). But granted the currency of Freudian theories, they were not taken seriously enough, at least in Spain, as critical tools for an understanding of the individual and of the culture until the early fifties. At that time in Germany and France (not to speak of the United States) psychoanalytic criticism had already achieved respectability.[2]

Spain's cultural lag in psychoanalytic criticism may be attributed to at least two causes. First, a manifest hostility to the movement was particularly prevalent during and after the Civil War when Freud and his disciples were thought to pose a serious threat to Christian values. Secondly, as some critics have maintained, a reticence, or even a resistance, to probe into the workings of the "dark side of life" and an inhibition before the sexual and intimate dimension of existence are peculiar to the Spanish character.[3] With these generalizations in mind, the following chapter will explore some Spanish views on psychoanalysis.

When one looks to the established figures in medicine and to the cultural critics of the twenties and thirties, Freud is either ignored, reviled or dismissed as a shaman and mystifier. Marañón, whose biological theories of male and female sexuality substantiate Freud's theses, is nevertheless, surprisingly frivolous about psychoanalysis. His contempt and petulance come through in statements like: "The fashion of Freud will pass like the fad for the tap-dance and the barbershop quartet. In fact, it might even disappear more quickly and permanently than these fads, and perhaps it is best that it does."[4] It is exceedingly surprising that the biologist F. Novoa-Santos, who between 1927 and 1931 wrote two speculative works on the death instinct, should not mention the name of Freud. In one of his books he does quote Fechner, who influenced Freud's *Beyond the Pleasure Principle* written in 1920. Reading Novoa's *La inmortalidad y los orígenes del sexo* (Madrid, 1931) one strongly suspects that he must have been familiar with Freud's classical study. Not only does he make reference to Fechner's homeostasis theory, but terms such as "nirvana principle" and the "fusion and diffusion of life and death instincts" occur. Of course, Novoa is unaware of the theory of repression and guilt, and therefore limits his study to a biological view of the instincts. Baroja, who was also a physician by training, took an instant dislike to psychoanalysis and dismissed it as another form of "Semitic mystification" attempting to subvert the purity of the scientific method.[5] Antonio Machado hardly discussed psychoanalysis, but when he finally did venture an opinion it was brief and to the point: when asked whether the analysis of trauma could render significant anthropological evidence, he simply replied "Bah!"[6]

Some artists, especially the surrealists, were deeply influenced by Freud. Vicente Aleixandre admits that his poetic phase of *Pasión de la tierra* owes its inspiration to Freud's work.[7] Salvador Dalí wrote a paper on paranoia and intrepidly sought an audience with the Father of Psychoanalysis—who was not impressed.[8] One of the best essays on the relationship between Freud and the surrealists was written by the critic and essayist Fernando Vela.[9] Freudian concepts were households words in intellectuals circles, but were used timidly and unsystematically. In literary criticism, with the exception of A. Valbuena Prat, who invokes Freud to explicate a text by Berceo (vol. I,

*Historia de la literatura española*) we must wait until the 1950s for a thoroughly psychoanalytic approach to literature and culture.

In the late thirties and early forties the principal contributors to psychoanalytic literature (though by no means exponents of the discipline) were López Ibor, Marco Merenciano and Laín Entralgo. Marco, who avoided polemics, wrote a fine analysis of the characters in the novels of Azorín as models of psychosomatic symptoms.[10] López Ibor, who dismissed Freudian theory as early as 1936, grudgingly learned to live with the success of psychoanalysis. López' continued hostility to the person of Freud and to psychoanalysis—specifically the metapsychology—will not escape the eye of the careful reader. His two "critical" studies of psychoanalysis are a travesty, a systematic evasion of the richest ideas Freud has to offer, not only by a deformation of his thought but by a substitution of *ad hominem* arguments for critical investigation, and tendentious commentary for sober evaluation.[11]

A more responsible, but not less hostile treatment is found in Laín Entralgo's study written in 1943. Laín begins his history of psychoanalysis with a study of verbal psychotherapy in classical Greece and the function and meaning of catharsis. But when he approaches the person and work of Freud, the study becomes marred by virulent outburst of personal prejudice—a reaction, no doubt, to the ideological threat of Freudianism that Laín, as a Catholic, must have felt in those years. This is unfortunate, because when he stops reminding us of Freud the "moral monster, resentful Jew and opportunist," Laín offers us a thorough phenomenological critique of psychoanalysis. He rejects Freudian hermeneutics, which he sees as an extension of positivistic techniques of reporting the irrational in the name of intentionality.[12] Laín asserts that the unconscious is simply not the center of one's biography: "Man interprets his own situation and makes his life through a series of choices because as a man he must make them. Man is by necessity a 'hermeneut' of himself."[13] Laín's critique of psychoanalysis owes much to Heidegger, Scheler, Bergson and Binswanger. To this must be added his vigilance for "error," a reflection of his apprehensions as a Catholic in Nationalist Spain which leads him to emphasize the destructive motives in the Freudian opus: ". . .negation of the primacy of the spirit postulated by Graeco-Christian thought; hostility to the logos. . .intellectual knowledge, spiritual love, and moral law."[14] Like Baroja, he attributes to Freud's theory of instincts a pseudo-scientific status of Semitic origin and concludes that "few movements in the history of thought have incurred errors as vulgar and dangerous as psychoanalysis."[15]

Expatriate Spaniards who have considered the cultural dimension of psychoanalysis are few. Ferrater Mora was the first to reveal the religious tonality of Freudianism, but he has never followed it up with a thorough critical study.[16] María Zambrano wrote an interesting essay on Freud, which is worth commenting upon briefly.[17] She distinguishes between Freud and Freudianism; the latter she labels an imposture. She credits Freud with a brilliant re-formulation of the idea that truth is revelation through his technique of dream-work, but reproaches him for his dogmatism. Freud reflects a period in history that has renounced the worth of reason; having banished the idea that man has a soul, he discovered that man is not made in the image of God, but is ruled by the blind, tragic force of libido, appetite, and will to power. By discovering the monster in man, Freud holds up the mirror to a creature who is a victim of sexual fury without hope of salvation. The three human qualities which Freud leaves out—love, purity, and reverence—Zambrano finds implicit in the Spanish myth par excellence: the Don Juan legend. On the surface, claims Zambrano, Don Juan is paradigmatic of man as sexual passion and will to power. But actually, Don Juan's actions only have meaning within the spiritual scope of Christian charity. Thus, the tragic sense of life, the life of blind passion, is redeemed by Doña Inés—the image of the immaculate conception by which Don Juan is freed from the tyranny of sexuality. Freudianism not only destroys the island of pure love amidst the furor of libido, but does away with the sacred principle of paternity as well; it is finally, the rejection of origins and of identity. It is a refusal to recognize our limitations and our historical responsibilities, a lack of humility and of trust. Without this guiding principle man can have no peace. Living in nature he experiences fear, a fear that engenders a deep anxiety and eventually leads to catastrophe. Freud, for Zambrano, is a witness of our times, a physician willing to cure and purify, but by reaching for the roots of evil he only made things worse.

This essay of María Zambrano's is important because it anticipates one of the central motifs of Rof Carballo's critique of culture: the notion of a "society without the father" and the erosion of the power of patriarchal symbolism, which is the subject of this chapter.

In addition to the work of Rof Carballo and Castilla del Pino, who are the subjects of this study, Domingo García Sabell and especially Luis Martín Santos have made significant contributions to psychoanalytic criticism. García Sabell is a physician and literary critic. His latest book *Tres síntomas de Europa* (Madrid: Revista de Occidente, 1969) is a psychoanalytic study of Van Gogh, James Joyce and Sartre. An auto accident in 1964 cut short the brilliant career of Luis Martín Santos whose novel *Tiempo de silencio* is an acknowledged landmark in post-war fiction. In his posthumous work *Libertad, temporalidad y transferencia en el psicoanálisis existencial* (Barcelona: Seix-Barral, 1964), Martín Santos combines psychoanalytic and phenomenological techniques to demonstrate that the notions of freedom and temporality have a dialectical function in human existence. And in *Apólogos* (Barcelona: Seix-Barral, 1970), a collection of unpublished essays and short stories, is a brief analysis of an anti-Don Juan myth among the Basques which the author calls the "Ramuncho complex."

## The Work of Juan Rof Carballo

Juan Rof Carballo was one of the few young medical students who in the early thirties was granted a fellowship to complete his studies in Europe. As a *pensionado* in Germany he enrolled at the universities of Cologne and Vienna where, between 1931-35, he studied biochemical pathology, neurology and general pathology. While at Vienna, Rof and his colleagues often passed the home of the legendary doctor Freud; but to most of them psychoanalysis, now past its sensational stage, remained a mere curiosity, divorced from their medical training and interests. Little did Rof realize in his Vienna days that twenty years later the works of Freud would be the theoretical source of his own medical anthropology. When he returned to Spain, Rof worked in close association with the two outstanding figures of Spanish medicine: Jiménez Díaz and Gregorio Marañón. In view of his extensive medical background, experience, and knowledge it is surprising that Rof had never been offered a post at the university. It is not too surprising, however, when one recalls the extreme politization and cliquishness, not to mention the archaism of the appointment system in Spain.

Around 1945 Rof became interested in medical anthropology through which he sought to fuse his training in biochemical pathology and a newly acquired interest in personal and social psychology. He was influenced by such American theorists as Cannon, Alexander, E. Erikson, Spitz and Sullivan. At the same time, he absorbed the ideas of the existential analysis schools headed by Binswanger and

Victor von Weizaecker, and the views of such orthodox Freudians as M. Bálint and G. Bally. To these influences we should add the constant and pervasive presence of two philosophers: Heidegger and Zubiri. Rof's medical anthropology is expounded in three principal works: *Patología psicosomática* (Madrid, 1949) *Cerebro interno y mundo emocional* (Madrid, 1952) and *Urdimbre afectiva y enfermedad* (Madrid, 1964). Laín Entralgo considers Rof to be a world authority on the psychological dimension of interpersonal relations. We will take note of some of the views of *Cerebro interno* and *Urdimbre* and their relation to myth and self-knowledge later in this study.

In addition to his contributions to psycho-biology and neurophysiology, Rof is the first genuine psychoanalytic critic of society and culture in contemporary Spanish letters. He was the first to notice and condemn the absence of serious psychoanalytic criticism in his country. He accused the Spanish writer of evading the richness and complexity of the subconscious, especially in women. With rare exceptions, claims Rof, the Spanish novelist avoids confrontation with the so-called dark powers of the psyche, and handles the subject of eroticism with unusual awkwardness and superficiality.

Against a generally hostile attitude toward psychoanalysis in the Spain of his time, the work of Rof stands out as a balanced but often timid approach to both Freudian and Jungian schools, whose theories he applies sparingly and undogmatically. Rof's eclecticism, his tendency to always synthesize, generalize and rework the ideas of wide and disparate sources, often buries his original line of thought and makes cumbersome reading. His most original essays, in which his psychoanalytic intuition prevails, or at least remains above the weight of authority, are the studies contained in *Entre el silencio y la palabra* (Madrid: Aguilar, 1960). It deals with the mythical motifs and symbolic expressions in the work of Rilke, Kierkegaard and Rosalía de Castro. Perhaps the best essay of the book is a study of superstition in Rof's native Galicia entitled "La santa compaña," in which he combines his analysis of native folklore with Freud's studies on melancholia to give a convincing and original explanation for the Galician's belief in the Procession of Souls. Also of special interest are Rof's character studies of Unamuno and Philip II.

## Method

The following sections consist of two parts. Part one is an exposition and explication of Juan Rof Carballo's anthropology and theory of culture based on his biological and psychoanalytic theories. Part two shows how, through the rhetoric of myth (traditional and creative) and other forms of figurative language, the intellectual content of these theories is enriched and transfused into a broader meaning which constitutes a view of life. In other words, we explore the function of myth as a rhetorical device which simultaneously affords additional imaginative insight into man's deepest levels of motivation, as well as his highest aspirations. Thus, in the essays under consideration, the structure of discourse known as myth is a mode of argumentation which relates biological and psychoanalytic notions to certain moral and religious assumptions: it complements an appeal to reason with an appeal to the imagination and belief, and supplements formal discourse with ethical proof.

I have isolated for the sake of analysis three categories of language in Rof's work: 1) the language of biology, 2) the language of psychoanalysis and 3) the language of myth. Each mode of discourse, although dependent upon the others, corresponds to a dimension of human existence and imparts explicitly or analogically an image of man and a set of personal values. Each category is a model of proof. The biological model, for example, provides formal proof of the fact that man's ability to reason and control the external world is rooted in the prolonged helplessness of his infancy. The psychoanalytic model conveys modern man's struggle for identity and self-knowledge, both of which are transformed by the rhetoric of myth into a spiritual meaning and a statement of values.

# 1. Anthropology

*The biological model*

Rof's chief contribution to psycho-biology and the empirical basis of his humanism is the theory of *urdimbre* which translates as "texture," "web," "weave," or "network." The author defines it as "a texture of transactional and reciprocal influences between mother and child from the moment of birth." By "transactional," Rof means not only mutual interaction, symbiosis, or dyad, but an influence of one party which, in itself, is continually being influenced in turn by the response it receives. This relationship involves a circular process which does not permit prediction or an a priori conception of which factors in the transaction will be decisive. The child's earliest disposition is modified by the reactions he awakens in the mother (or substitute tutelar figures) and vice-versa. Human beings are particularly receptive to these tutelar imprints because, unlike other higher animals, man is notably premature at birth and thus more susceptible to transactional and programming influences.[18] Rof has often embellished this notion of *urdimbre* with mythical allusions, comparing the weave or web to the Fates.

There are three basic *urdimbres* which determine the structure of personality: the constitutive or primary, the *urdimbre* of order, and the *urdimbre* of identity. The first one is decisive in character formation and is woven in the first months of life; it will condition all subsequent psychic development: affective relationships, personal preferences, style of life, world view, etc., all of which are rooted and shaped in this first transactional relationship. The *urdimbre* of order, although incipient from the beginning and coextensive with the primary *urdimbre*, becomes prominent in the fourth or fifth year of life. At this stage, the child incorporates the social norms and moral patterns that will influence the choice of his personal values. Above all, it organizes a hierarchical world for the child which serves as a basis for the development of a conscious sense of values as well as the superego (unconscious). Rof emphasizes the difference between conscious morality and automatic obedience. Finally, the *urdimbre* of identity appears in adolescence (cf. Erikson) when the individual must confront his self-image with the concept others have of him and forge an authentic self. More will be said about this *urdimbre* later on.

The three *urdimbres* interact and overlap from the very beginning of life and are conditioned considerably by genetic factors. In addition, *urdimbre* has the following characteristics and functions. It is first of all *programmatic*; it equips the child with a set pattern of behavior in very much the same way as one would "program" a computer. It is *psychosocial* because it determines the unconscious mechanisms that appear in the individual's choices in friendship, marriage, career, etc. It is also characteristic of *urdimbre* to be *transmissional* whereby cultural patterns are passed on from generation to generation. Rof emphasizes that the weave of the *urdimbre* is never complete; although tutelar influences and structures protect and fortify the individual, they also imprison and truncate the personality (i.e. narcissistic mother, tyrannical super-ego). In the struggle for identity, man may react in various ways to his primary *urdimbre*, which may be a source of rebellion, overcompensation, or self-discovery.

The two most important functions of *urdimbre* are that of bond (*urdimbre vinculadora*) and of basic trust (*urdimbre de confianza*). The first function designates the transmission of behavioral patterns from previous generations and constitutes the social and racial strata of personality. But, above all, it provides the individual with a *sense of tradition*. The *urdimbre* of trust refers to those primary transactions which decide whether the external world is harmonious, coherent and purposeful, or labyrinthine, chaotic and absurd. The *urdimbre* of trust is the biological substratum of hope. When this essential interaction between mother and child is defective, the individual acquires a propensity for vagabondage, aggression, delinquency, despair, sado-masochism and inverted values.

The transactional mechanisms involved in the formation of bond and trust, and the consequences of their deficiency in character development, is studied by Rof in a brief analysis of the life and work of Nerval, Baudelaire, Sartre and Genet. In all, he finds either a passive, weak, inert, or totally absent mother and a substitute father figure. In Baudelaire and Sartre where the absence of the father did not allow for the development of the super-ego, the usual struggle for identity against the paternal image was passed by. Instead they confronted a vicarious father (General Aupick, Schweitzer) who could be despised with impunity. Both men also felt themselves to be the sons of a "servant-mother" (humiliated and spineless) which produced in them a contempt for tradition.[19]

Defective primary transactions in the childhood of Baudelaire and Sartre are also manifest in the obsessive anti-natural symbolism of their work. It is well known that the French poet abhorred "nature" and that Sartre's work abounds in nausea and general disgust before the plain facticity of the external world. Sartre's ultimate trust, suggests Rof, is not man or the cosmos, but the power of words. At the conclusion of this essay, we are told that these artists offer a classic paradox in human nature: that man's intelligence is rooted in his essential neediness and helplessness (*menestrosidad*). In the cases of Baudelaire, Sartre and Genet, intelligence defiantly and diabolically revolts against that which has given them the staff of their humanity: personal roots and a sense of tradition. Later on, we shall see how this rejection of roots and inversion of values through the power of intelligence, constitutes for Rof the source of man's spiritual malady.

## Conservative Humanism

*The mythical model: a Promethean interpretation of the Oedipus legend*

If the biological model emphasized the mother-child relationship, the mythical paradigm (psychoanalytic model) has a double purpose: to dramatize man's struggle for identity and to save the father figure from the deterministic, negative and destructive meaning imposed on it by Freud's notion of the superego. The Oedipus myth is not, for Rof, primarily an unconscious projection of the incest wish, but is essentially a Promethean myth. The notion that Oedipus' weakness lies not in his libido but in a lack of self-awareness and a "will to non-truth" was formulated by Rof years before Paul Ricoeur developed it in his study of Freud.[20] However, since Rof's main rhetorical themes are the figurative meanings of the sense of sight, and the concepts of unveiling, deciphering, demystification of the self, and spiritual regeneration, he is heavily indebted to Ricoeur's double hermeneutic of "suspicion" and of "belief." The hermeneutic of suspicion exposes a "false consciousness" by revealing the pitfalls of rationalism and showing that man is always something other than what he thinks he is. It deciphers the archaic structure of personality which stands in the way of spiritual development. But to this *regressive* mode of interpretation Ricoeur adds a progressive mode. Implicit in the *archeology* of the subject is a hermeneutic of belief, a *teleology*, the power that moves him toward self-fulfillment and an appropriation of the pristine and authentic meaning of the symbol(s) that guide his spiritual adventure. Once man has interpreted and unveiled the archaic "phantasm" of his personality, or, once he has understood (seen), he is ready to hear the word, the message that the symbol imparts.[21]

What Ricoeur is saying is that the Oedipus complex need not vitiate the transcendent meaning of the father figure. This is of central importance in Rof, for whom a sense of personal identity and fullness of personality is ineluctably tied to the generative, foundational and numinous symbolism associated with the myths of patriarchy.

With these preliminary considerations in mind we can now explore Rof's concern for the diminishing role of the father figure in contemporary society. We will begin by focusing attention first on Rof's analysis of the Oedipus legend.

Rof has conscientiously catalogued the myths contained in the Oedipus legend.[22] One of them, correlative to his theory of primary *urdimbre*, is the Segismundo complex—the myth of the abandoned child—named after the prince of Calderón's *La vida es sueño* who is confined from birth to a tower and is thus bereft of all tutelage. Segismundo is a symbolic personification of man without roots or tradition. Since he lacked the constitutive and mediating agency of other human beings, he is unable to discern dreams from reality. The Segismundo complex is a derivative of the Oedipus legend and is an extrapolation or imaginative conceptualization of a defective (in this case non-existent) primary *urdimbre*. We can also consider it, therefore, as an ethical proof corresponding to the biological model discussed above.

More important for Rof is the Promethean myth and the myth of Tiresias implicit in the Oedipus legend. It will be remembered that Tiresias attempts to dissuade Oedipus from his determination to find out why the city is being devasted by the plague. But Oedipus is the man who must find out the truth at all costs, hence Holderlin's observation that Oedipus had one eye too many. But, ironically enough, says Rof, Oedipus was blind even before he put out his eyes. Did he not ignore the warning of the oracle that he was destined to kill his father and marry his mother? Why didn't he return to his native land to find out who in fact were his parents and thereby avoid his fate? It seems, continues Rof, that this man, whose intelligence and passion for truth had conquered the Sphinx (the unconscious; the devouring mother), was ignorant and blind to that aspect of truth which concerned him most and which should have been the most obvious to him. If Oedipus had one eye too many, he was also partially blind. From this Rof deduces the moral that "we only see through our blindness."

The prophet Tiresias is also blind, that is, he is blind to the world around him, but has the power to foretell the future. Rof fuses his exegeses of the Promethean and Tiresias myths into a general conclusion about human nature:

> The closer we come to truth the more it escapes us, the more we evade another truth as important as the first. The hubris which falls on the arrogance of the man who steals the fire from the gods, the Promethean man, has here another meaning: all knowledge condemns us to an ignorance of another important aspect of truth. Insight into certain arcane secrets is paid by an obtuse blindness to the most obvious.

> Cuánto más nos acercamos a la verdad, más se escabulle, más se nos escapa otra verdad tan importante como la primera. La "hybris" que cae sobre la arrogancia del hombre que arranca el fuego de los dioses,

del hombre prometeico, tiene aquí otra expresión: todo saber condena a la ignorancia de otro importante sector de la verdad. La clarividencia para ciertos arcanos y remotos secretos se paga con un obtusa ceguera para lo más próximo.[23]

## A historicist interpretation

The method of interpretation applied to the Promethean myth is not psychoanalytic but existential-historicist. The hubris alluded to is the evolution in Western consciousness of atheist humanism. A Promethean reading of the Oedipus legend becomes, for Rof, a metaphor for the negative values of contemporary culture and the ethical leitmotif of his essays. The existential meaning of blindness is Western man's irresponsible use of technology, a knowledge and mastery that have brought about the destruction of nature and alienation of man from himself and from others. The moral implications of this hubris is the arrogance born of an intoxicating will to power and the "idolatry of the self." The religious meaning of hubris is for Rof as for Laín Entralgo (see Chapter II) a deification of the self, a "vital arrogance" which refuses to acknowledge dependence on a higher order of being.

## Displacement of the super-ego

The subjection of the mythical model to existential and religious modes of analysis is particularly evident in Rof's study of the role of aggression in contemporary culture. An historicist reading of aggression will now displace the Freudian view of an externalization and projection of guilt feelings originating in an over-demanding and punitive super-ego. Rof does not deny that the repressions and renunciations imposed by authority can generate guilt and violence, but he does consider the orthodox Oedipal dynamic a secondary factor in the formation of aggression. In fact, he is more concerned with preserving the super-ego (a demystified one) as the foundation of social order and the source of the sacred. Furthermore, he imputes to modern man's Promethean arrogance the destruction in our time of the viability of both patriarchal and matriarchal (chthonic) symbolism. We begin to see now that Rof owes very little to Freud. It is to Heidegger, Zubiri and Neumann (a disciple of Jung) that he will look for an explanation of aggression consonant with his ethico-religious beliefs.

Rof himself says that he prefers a historicist view of aggression and thereby devalues its libidinal source in favor of a conscious strata of motivation. Following Heidegger he sees modern man's will to non truth, his ironical passion for knowledge, as a perversion of thought: the substitution of *calculating,* dehumanizing thought, proper of technology, for *meditative* or contemplative thought which reflects man's essential humanity. This "will to non-truth" has not only undermined the patriarchal structure of society with all its coercive and regulative functions, but has closed man in his most radical pride. "Never has contemporary man, so proud of his knowledge about the world, , actually know less about spiritual matters."[24] Those who would attribute the increase of violent behavior in our time to an innate aggressive instinct released by the super-ego exaggerate: "Surely the worst kind of violence is not innate aggression, but the aggression that being outside of man has been blindly set on a course beyond control."[25] But is this aggression which threatens civilization, and which Freud traced to the fatal opposition between Eros and Thanatos, a fully conscious phenomenon for Rof? Is it purely the product of wrong thinking? Is it born of arrogance and pride? Or does it also have an unconscious component in which the dynamics are different from Freud's notion of instinctual dualism? Rof also writes that "man's cruelty, his destructive aggressiviness, his incredible violence, stem, like the power of his intelligence, from his radical helplessness."[26] This seem to suggest that there is a link between the primary *urdimbre* (man's origins, tradition) and the notion of hubris which corresponds to man's struggle for identity. That is, man becomes anti-socially aggressive first because of a lack of care or deficient transaction in early childhood and secondly because he absolutizes the value of operational reason (knowledge in the service of the will to power). There is, then, an unconscious, as well as a conscious source of aggression. Where does this leave the problem of guilt and its role in the expression of violence?

Unfortunately, Rof never tells why he rejects the Freudian thesis on the relationship between guilt and aggression described in *Civilization and Its Discontents.* He prefers a Jungian, typological or stratified theory of guilt which is more consonant with his own concept of the three *urdimbres.* There are primary, secondary and tertiary types of guilt. A primary form of guilt results from the anxiety of object-loss experienced in a defective transaction of a constitutive *urdimbre* (i.e. a child feels unwanted, that the mother "will not return," and therefore feels guilty). This primary guilt becomes the substratum for the super-ego formed during the *urdimbre* of order. If the child feels that the "mother will return" and has some assurance of being loved then the super-ego will be a positive element in the development of personal identity. On the other hand, if there is no sense of trust established between mother and child or if the former is too rigid, cold or distant, the child, searching for order and meaning, may develop a cruel and tyrannical super-ego which sets in motion a secondary guilt. This secondary guilt, nurtured by an overdemanding super-ego, is not accountable for civilization's discontents, although it does contribute to it. The crucial guilt is derived from the struggle for identity whose negative psychological, social and religious expressions correspond in Rof's anthropology to man's four fundamental passions: idolatry of the self, insatiable wants, the need for admiration, and the impulse to dominate and enslave. These passions, in turn, correspond to four deadly sins: pride, avarice, vanity, and the destruction of the sacred identity of our fellow man.[27] What then is tertiary guilt? If primary guilt stems from a defective mother-child relationship and if the super-ego corresponds to a secondary guilt, a tertiary form of guilt evolves from a conscious assassination of God, or what in our time, since Nietzsche, has been knowm as the "death of God." For Rof, the struggle for identity bring into play the fundamental passions of man, including the hubris of knowledge and self-deification, and their expression in calculated thinking or the will to power manifest in the idolatry of Science. It is this conscious murder of God which produces an unconscious guilt.[28]

One can now understand the link between the concept of self-knowledge, the primary *urdimbre* and the struggle for identity. One can likewise comprehend the relation between man's origins and his destiny, between the vicissitudes of his infancy and the notion of hubris (self-deification). Man's intelligence, his ability to create and destroy, his radical pride, are rooted in the helplessness and neediness *(menestrosidad)* of his childhood. This basic indigence, when exacerbated by deficient transaction of a primary *urdimbre* can, in the struggle for identity, take the form of either unmitigated violence, or of an overcompensatory, critical, negative intelligence which, through an inversion of values, absolutizes reason and deifies the self.

One of the main weaknesses of Rof's theory becomes apparent at this juncture. He fails to differentiate between a critical intelligence, which manifests itself as an inversion of values such as anti-theism and nihilism (Sartre) and the hubris of science which assumes the form of operational reason and is proper of technology. Both may stem from an anthropological hubris but they are not necessarily interdependent. When critical intelligence is employed in the service of metaphysical revolt, as in Camus, for example, it is, even when vehemently anti-traditional and anti-theistic, a reaction against scientism and consequent dehumanization. This is a self-conscious intelligence, prepared to correct itself. On the other hand, the hubris of calculating reason is blind, alienated "rationalization."

To return to our main theme, Promethean arrogance according to Rof is not only a gesture of ingratitude and a revolt against that which constitutes the ground and source of our being, but a repudiation of tradition woven in the primary *urdimbre*. For this reason, Rof derives two myths from the Oedipus legend. The myth of Segismundo (the abandoned child) and the Promethean myth of man as the will to non-truth acquire full meaning in man's struggle for identity (self-affirmation) which, in our time, has taken the form of "the double castration of the symbols of matriarchy (destruction of nature) and patriarchy (forgetfulness of Being, refusal to recognize God as the ground of Being)."[29] This double assassination or "castration" is a further indication that modern man has the pretension of being an Adam and that he will not recognize his debt to the past. Man should recognize his debt, and gratefully become aware of the forces that shaped him even if these forces are negative. Thus:

> When Sartre affirms. . .that "the bond of paternity is rotten," he commits two errors: first, he does not realize that his opinions have an emotional base secretly rooted in the vicissitudes of his childhood; secondly, he does not notice that it is this blindness which conditions his unique type of critical intelligence and the peculiarly desolate and negating aspect of his creativity. Consequently, even "supressed" and "negated," this paternity continues to be, for him, to some extent, still luminous.

> De ahí que cuando Sartre afirma. . .que es el "vínculo de la paternidad," el que "está podrido," comete dos errores: el uno, no darse cuenta de que sus opiniones tienen un trasfondo emocional enraizado secretamente con las viscisitudes de su infancia; el otro, no advertir que es esta ceguera la que condiciona su tipo especial de inteligencia crítica y hasta el peculiar matiz desolado y negador de su capacidad creadora. Por consiguiente, aun aparentemente "suprimida" y "negada", esta paternidad sigue siendo en él, en cierto modo, todavía luminosa.[30]

This lack of reverence for origins, this absence of awe before that mysterious power of love and care which permits man to exist and equips him with his peculiar way of perceiving and structuring reality, constitutes for Rof an impoverishment of the person. He reminds us that Freud, who claimed to know nothing about Judaism and certainly did not practice it, nevertheless confessed that perhaps what constituted his most radical self, his identity, was his Jewishness. The power of imagination and that of intelligence which have forged the great monuments to civilization are rooted in that *tremendum* of the primary *urdimbre,* which is enigmatically linked to the realm of the numinous. Modern man's willful destruction of Nature, the source of all matriarchal symbolism (earth, care, tenderness, fecundity), his assassination of God and his resolution to live in a "society without the father," or without foundations, transcendence and ultimate identity, is experienced as a *loss,* and an impoverishment of being. Atheism is the ultimate expression of this impoverishment and the religious significance of man's will to non-truth. Here Rof is in full agreement with Zubiri for whom atheism is a form of existence that is incapable of fathoming its own source. The atheist denies his dependence on the source of all being, but he denies it by affirming it through a process of self-deification, the deification of his person in which he identifies being with his own life.[31]

## The Hermeneutics of Restoration

It is a mistake to believe, admonishes Rof, that a fortification of the ego through a secular pedagogy, administered in the spirit of enlightenment, will enable man to accept the "reality principle" and dispense with a need for the father. It is equally misleading to reduce the function of the father figure to his authority, his hostility to the matriarchal world or to confuse his divine image with the super-ego, derived from cultural canons.[32] Freud, continues Rof, saw in the super-ego only a coercive force opposed to instinctual gratification, which consequently cripples the development of the person. Under the tyranny of this negative super-ego which enlists automatic obedience, the experience of the sacred also becomes restricted to an authoritarian, over-demanding, and cruel deity which imprisons man in a vicious circle of guilt and persecutory violence. Rof attempts to show that there is a more basic, authentic, life-enhancing, and universal function of the father-image which is indestructible and cannot be replaced by a mature, critical ego, or by an adjustment to the reality-principle. Beneath the slow but persistent struggle of reason, which hopes to free humanity from the idols of its fears, there is another power which Freud unconsciously deified: Eros, the force that holds together all things and is somehow connected—although Freud never suspected it—to the God of the Gospels.[33] To illustrate this oversight (blindness) on the part of Freud, Rof quotes Paul Ricoeur's observation that in *Totem and Tabu* the author ignores the implications of the fraternal pact in which the brothers forbid themselves the repetition of their horrendous crime. Must the sons (humanity) become the fatal victims of "the return of the repressed"? Or, can this bond among the brothers become a symbol of the restorative power of Eros which, as the power of faith and love, can overcome the tyranny of the super-ego?

For Rof, the parental figures are central in the development of the personality: "In the depths of the human soul are the two nuclei of personal crystalization, the protective image of the mother, which the individual will rediscover as the source of tradition, and the guiding influence of the father."[34] The symbolic power of the father is tremendous. As progenitor he is the source of "the will to found" (foundation) of institutions and of the group. "Man is always dependent on some kind of supra- or trans-personal structure which enables him to create, to build and to integrate himself into a group."[35] The instinct to build *(fundar)* is inextricable from man's essential humanity.

But the father is also the symbol of "the superior," "the celestial," and "the principle of harmony and order." He is also "that which is" and makes possible "what may be." In short, God as the father remits us to the ground of Being. What, then, is the ultimate significance of the "rebellion against the father" and the "death of God?"

> Essentially, the present "rebellion against the father," or rather, the intellectual consciousness of this rebellion as a phase in the history of man, reveals a psychological and sociological phenomenon which Heidegger named "the neglect of Being."
> . . . . . . . . . . . . . . . . . . . . . . . . . . . . . . . . . . . . . . . . . . . . . . . . . . . . . . . . . . . . . . .
> The reduction of the problem of religion to the "question of the father" is a simplification determined ultimately by unconscious anxieties and by the incapacity to deal with the problem of Being in all its transcendence.
>
> En el fondo, la actual "rebelión contra el padre," o mejor dicho, la conciencia intelectual de esa rebelión como una fase de la historia del hombre, hace aflorar a la psicología y a la sociología el "olvido del Ser" del que habla Heidegger.[36]
> . . . . . . . . . . . . . . . . . . . . . . . . . . . . . . . . . . . . . . . . . . . . . . . . . . . . . . . . . . . . . . .
> La reducción del problema de la religión a la "cuestión del padre" es, por tanto, una simplificación, determinada en su último trasfondo por angustias subconcientes y por la incapacidad de abordar, en toda

su trascendencia, el problema del sentido del Ser.[37]

The meaning of the Promethean version of the Oedipus legend is now obvious: The modern revolt against patriarchal and matriarchal structures of personality evolves from the aberrant expression of the struggle for identity. If identity implies self-knowledge, then Promethean knowledge, manifest in Science and Technology, at the service of the will to power, is ignorance, for it has reduced man's potential to be truly human. Progress, the hubris of Western man, is knowledge but not wisdom, power but not the enrichment of the person. It has given society more and more things but less and less Being.

Since Rof virtually appropiates Ricoeur's teleological hermeneutic to restore the authentic possibilities of the father image, I will not repeat it here. It would be more instructive to say a few words about Rof's restoration of matriarchal symbolism by applying this regressive-progressive hermeneutic to Freud's concept of sublimation. The reductive method in psychoanalysis, according to Rof, is incapable of disclosing, in symbols of sublimation, a meaning other than that of sexuality. The kiss and the caress, for example, can be submitted to both a psychoanalytic and phenomenological interpretation. Both could be the sublimated expressions of the sexual impulse; but then how do we explain its repeated use in social and religious ceremony? The kiss and the caress are *not reducible* to a basically sexual meanning, they are also instruments of tenderness and the essential components of tutelage and care which form a healthy person. It is this very tenderness which helps to dissipate a form of innate aggression which could prove dangerous. In the kiss, says Rof, "man repeats his infancy, but this is a regression other than that observed in psychotherapy; it is rather a *re-progression,* an exercise in a symbolic function which returns man to the moment when motherly care and protection opened to him the light of the spirit. This same symbol (the kiss) now opens to him mysteriously a world of a transcendent order: the world of love from which everything springs."[38]

If, behind the symbol of the father as a coercive and punitive deity, Ricoeur's double hermeneutic has uncovered the possibility of a teleology of the spirit which, in a second naiveté, is able to call to a God of love, so Rof's restorative interpretation leaves man at the portals of childhood where he may discover the world of tenderness in the perennial symbol of the mother.

Ricoeur has warned that "one is never certain that a given symbol of the sacred is not simply the return of the repressed" and that the archaic structure of personality is indestructible. But, as Rof would emphatically agree, this does not exhaust the meaning of the religious symbol, which is, as the father figure suggests, "over-determined." Thus, "the father figure signifies regeneration; birth analogously stands for rebirth; the childhood which is behind me—signifies the other childhood, the second naiveté."[39]

## Language and Silence

Finally, a few words need to be said on the importance of language in Rof's anthropology. In a recent article he wrote that psychoanalysis is not only, as Ricoeur would have it, a hermeneutic, but also, from the therapist's point of view, a maieutic by which the patient can be helped to "bring to light his own truth."[40] This therapeutic midwifery is more than the traditional language of psychotherapy based on interpretation of the spoken word. The standard form of analysis considers what Rof (following Bálint) calls the "Oedipal zone" or a triangular relationship in which the patient verbalizes a problem stemming from his Oedipal conflict. The verbalization of neurosis corresponds to the stratum in his character development or *urdimbre* in which the individual has incorporated the cultural values of his group, one of which is obviously language. Next, there is a pre-verbal or bi-personal zone open to analysis which corresponds to a more basic, instinctual stratum of *urdimbre* in which personal traits are transmitted not by word, as in the Oedipal phase, but through the mute language of gesture, habit and attitude of mother-child transaction. This more primitive stage is not characterized by conflict but by *need*. Therefore, when this need is transferred to the doctor, the function of language (concepts, interpretations, ideas) becomes unimportant. What does matter is the expressive content of the relationship by which the individual's primary need will become manifest as *a need to develop and complete his person.*[41]

There is still a "third zone" of the psychic structure of which very little is known and must, therefore, be approached intuitively. This is the zone of solitude and silence. "If in the Oedipal relation, language was the form of communication, and if in the dual relationship it was pre-verbal. . .now there is no communication. Instead, there is something more important than it first appears to be: silence."[42] Implicit in this silence is the seed of creativity and the capacity for recovery. To Rof, silence is a chtonic symbol that encompasses the generative processes of Nature which, in its stillness, weaves the first strand of life. By analogy, silence can impart on the patient an understanding richer than words can express. It can also be a beginning of a creative process that will be his own cure when, in the patient's solitude, this deep understanding will reach fruition. Rof concludes that, ultimately, man should be able to endure in his maturity the rewarding burden of solitude: the precondition of *Befindlichkeit* of all creativity.

In summary, then, the philosophical tenor of Rof's concept of man and culture runs counter to the principal tenets of Freudian matapsychology. For, whereas Freud conceived the individual as opposed to and in conflict with society, Rof shows that man could not exist and subsist, that he could not become truly a man, without his constitutive relation with others—the group which receives him and equips him with a world. Man is a creature of conflict, but more basically he is a creature of need. During the process of hominization, two factors are eminently suitable to fill man's need: tradition and an openness to transcendence (God). Now, we can focus our attention to myth as a rhetoric of humanism in the work of Rof.

## 2. Myth as Rhetoric

*Paradox as drama and wisdom*

The central image in the work of Rof is the blindness of Oedipus. Its metaphysical and moral significance is dramatized by a recourse to the paradox that "we see through our blindness." This concept is reinforced with ancillary anthropological paradoxes such as the contingency of power on helplessness, intelligence on need, and liberty on limitation and imprisonment. The function of paradox here is "to make us see more clearly," to give us a privileged insight into the human condition. Paradox as a figure of thought provides, by an association of antithetical concepts and a juxtaposition of contradictory notions, an existential rather than a formal proof. "We see through our blindness" is an aphoristic, synthetic paradox. It is not a formal epistemological contradiction which begs a solution; it is not an analytic exposure of incompatibilities, but a summary intuitive statement which captures an essentially human problem and relates it to the ultimate meaning of existence. Thus, it is an insight which passes from mere knowledge to wisdom where the form of expression is ultimately imagistic: the anthropomorphic examples or symbolic per-

sonifications of Oedipus, Prometheus and Segismundo. These names
not only add a universal dimension to the paradoxical sight-blind-
ness, but their creative use provides a sense of drama as symbolic
meaning that is proyected on contemporary history. The drama con-
sists of modern man playing out unwittingly the act of self-destruc-
tion with the very instruments that have freed him from bondage. The
dramatic power of the Promethean myth increases as Rof attempts to
show how, in the Western tradition, man's will to self-deification
("will to non-truth") corresponds paradoxically to his self-alienation.
Myth is the expression of this insight.

## The negative example of Prometheus-Oedipus

By attributing a negative example to the figure of Prometheus,
Rof attacks the basic anthropological premises of atheistic human-
ism. The concept of hubris is clearly subordinated to the Christian
image of man; this becomes quite evident when Rof links man's strug-
gle for identity to four of the seven deadly sins. The negative view of
Prometheus is reinforced with two kinds of arguments: the argument
*ad hominem* and the omission of alternatives.

When Unamuno wished to show that Spinoza's rationalism was
only a feeble attempt to disguise his hunger for inmortality he was
employing the *ad hominem* argument. The main question for Una-
muno was not the consistency and coherence of the *Ethics,* but: Was
Spinoza happy? At two crucial points in *Violencia y ternura* Rof uses
the *ad hominem* argument against two of the most formidable ration-
alists of our time: Freud and Sartre. His aim, as we have seen earlier,
is to dramatize with very specific examples the theme that "we see
through our blindness." The *ad hominem* argument here is a device
whereby the critic goes beyond the writer's own explanation and
seeks evidence from the example of his life. The critic's point is that
his subject's life contradicts or is inconsistent with his professed be-
liefs, or that he doesen't *see* the deeper implications of his own ideas.
This is why the *ad hominem* argument is perhaps the ethical argu-
ment par excellence. By shifting the focus from intellectual
content to motives, it asks for accountability and justification and
thus for Rof it further demonstrates man's paradoxical nature. Here
is Rof's argument against Freud:

> When asked what constituted for him human happiness Freud ans-
> wered laconically: to love and work. Why then did he overlook in his
> answer the very thing he was doing, the very essence of his life, the

73

very center of his existence? Which was to *found* a school, to *create* a new science, to *give birth* to an enlightening system.

> A la pregunta de en qué consistía para él la felicidad humana. . .Freud responde lacónicamente: *Lieben und Arbeiten,* esto es, amar y trabajar. ¿Por qué en esta respuesta olvidó precisamente aquello que él estaba haciendo, que constituía la esencia de su vida, el núcleo más entrañable de su existir? Que era *fundar* una escuela, *crear* una ciencia nueva, *dar luz* a un sistema esclarecedor.[43]

Rof argues that Freud possibly repressed the feminine component of his character because he was blind to man's generative function. This he explains by citing the rigidly patriarchal structure of the society in which he lived and the peculiar family and racial background which influenced his personality. At any rate, it is not what Freud said about the meaning of life and happiness but how he failed to see the ultimate meaning of what he said. He theoretically repudiated the sacred meaning of human origin and undermined the reverential status of authority and tradition; but in life, claims Rof, he affirmed these very values. Likewise, Sartre's statement that "the bonds of paternity are rotten" is turned against Sartre when Rof wants to show that it is precisely this negative attitude, this blindness to the fundamental meaning and function of paternity, which accounts for Sartre's unique intellect whereby he unwittingly affirms the function of paternity.

With the *ad hominem* argument Rof reiterates the themes of paradox, blindness and arrogance. By paradox Rof hopes to show that pure reason is blind to the ultimate meaning of existence. Paradox as wisdom embarrasses reason and shames intellectual arrogance (blindness).

The omission of alternatives is an often-used rhetorical device in Rof's essays, although it is not as common as the *ad hominem* argument. Rof emphasizes that the father image or an image of the deity derived from the super-ego is not the *real* authentic symbol but an archaic, infantile residue projected on the father or deity. But Rof does not concede this standard of authenticity to reason. That is, if calculating or operational reason proper to technology is not distinctly human reason, but an aberrant manifestation of the will to power, then meditative reason is authentically human reason. However, admission on the part of Rof is deceptive because unless meditative reason is subordinated to religious values it remains anthropologically indistinguishable from calculating reason. In short, any mode of reason which remains centered in man alone is an alienated form of reason. Whereas religious symbolism can regain its ground through a process of demystification, the recovery of the authentic (human) function of reason still remains only a handmaiden of *religion*. While Rof frequently echoes Heidegger's notion that only meditative reason can restore a mode of being which could properly be called human, he does not really mean it, or at least he only agrees with Heidegger in part. For Rof the only consequential alternative for human reason is to recognize its limitations.

## Myth as rhetoric

For Freud, myth (the Oedipus complex) served the function of enhancing his "reductionist" conclusions about the nature of man. By invoking the Oedipus legend Freud dramatizes the anthropological meaning of his process of the "deconversion" of the sacred, at the end of which religion is ultimately reduced to a morbid elaboration of an archaic trauma. Rof, on the other hand, inspired by Ricoeur's hermeneutics of a teleology of the spirit, uses myth to bring us closer to what he considers the authentic meaning of the sacred symbols of Christianity. Rof's rhetoric of humanism consists precisely in his re-creation or re-interpretation of traditional myths, as well as the creation of a new myth—such as the Segismundo complex—which serves as a critique of contemporary culture and the ethical proof of his anthropology.

The function of creative myth, as Joseph Campbell reminds us, "is to reconcile waking consciousness to the *mysterium tremendum et fascinans* of this universe as it is and to render an interpretative total image of the same, as known to contemporary consciousness."[44] But the expression of this total, integrating vision can rest either at the limits of secular truth (i.e. Joyce's *Ulysses*) or point the way to a religious symbol. Rof leaves us at the portals of Christian (Catholic) symbolism arguing in the analogical language of biology, psychoanalysis and myth that the revealed truth of his faith is the fulfillment and ultimate meaning of man's spiritual odyssey. We are asked, in short, to take that leap of faith which links our scientific and philosophical understanding of ourselves to universal religious symbols. By exploring the positive functions of the father figure and dramatizing its anthropological importance by recourse to the Oedipus-Prometheus myths, Rof offers proof by analogy of a necessity for belief if man "is to be fully a man." Likewise, the Segismundo myth is an imaginative reconstruction, a negative example, a dramatization of the importance of primary *urdimbre,* and an argument by analogy for tradition. Segismundo actually symbolizes spiritual autonomy (atheism) as well as the repudiation of the great cultural myths of the West:

> Modern man resists desperately the recognition of his dependence on the source and ground of all Being *(de estar religado).* Because he no longer belongs to a tradition of great myths, he wants to belong at all costs to "little myths" (i.e. political parties) and dreams of a social paradise. . . .He stubbornly insists in being a Segismundo.

> El hombre actual se resiste desesperadamente a dejar de estar religado. Por eso, porque ha dejado de pertenecer a una tradición de grandes mitos, quiere pertenecer a otros mitos pequeñitos. . .y sueña con un paraíso social. . . .Se resiste a ser Segismundo.[45]

Myth is the imaginative organization of modern experience, and Rof's choice of symbolic personification is meant to communicate a meaning of loss or "the impoverishment of the person." But this symbolism can also be identified with an order of motivation extrinsic to the immediate meaning of the myth itself, whereby a negative meaning is rhetorically analogous to the religious stratum of symbols. Thus, patriarchy is analogous to God and is mediated by the Oedipus-Prometheus motif; chthonic mythology is analogous to tradition and is mediated by the Segismundo myth.

*The uses of analogy*

In addition to the analogical function of myth, Rof's biological and psychoanalytic language also points to an order of meaning outside the literal and formal content of scientific discourse proper to its discipline, that is, its language is not always univocal. Biology, like any other science, often borrows its terms from other sciences, from philosophy and from ordinary language—which does not exclude, of course, figurative language. This figurative language in Rof's anthropology conveys not only a meaning peculiar to biology, but, like myth, refers to an underlying and pervasive spiritual meaning which the author attributes to it. The language of biology, or at least some of its terms or concepts, function analogously. When speaking of the analogical function of biology I mean that a higher order or principle is expressed in a lower form. The notion of *urdimbre,* for example, is a biological concept correlative to *predestination.* This is not an arbitrary correlation. I have given an account of the numerous functions of *urdimbre* as a miraculous, enigmatic biological phenomenon which decides, weaves, seals, and determines the individual's fate; yet Rof speaks of it in the context of the necessity and desirability of human freedom, and gives it a theological dimension.

The psychoanalytic notion of aggression, which for Rof is both conscious and unconscious, is quite compatible with Augustine's *libido dominandi*. Ancillary to the idea of aggression is the psychoanalytic concept of the "struggle for identity" which is clearly identified with arrogance and intellectual *pride*.

Rof's questionable psychoanalysis of Sartre may also be clasified as an argument by analogy. Sartre's repudiation of paternity, his self-affirmation through a negation of origins, is really an argument against atheism. It is but a variant of Zubiri's theory that the atheist can only affirm his existence (ground his being) in his own person through a negative relationship to God.

## Rof's imagery

We have seen that the biological and psychoanalytic models and mythical paradigms converge finally on a note of awe and reverence before the mystery of human origins and their relationship to the numinous. Rof conveys this mystery and drama of "hominization" with evolutionist imagery that is reminiscent of Teilhard de Chardin:

> Huddled in one of those corners far from the battling anthropoid tribes, a mother is attempting to nurse her offspring which today we would call a "super-seven-month child." Man is born as a seven-month child, as an imperfect, abortive being who with that margin of care and luck is able to barely survive and disguise his abnormality. The abnormality of this "australoid" lies in his extreme prematurity. Millons of them were exterminated by circumstances, the hostile climate, or by their parents who were irritated at having given birth to a biologically inferior child. But why within this harsh "law of the jungle" does there appear another equally important law whereby the more helpless and weak a living being is, the more interest there is in preserving its life? An archaic mystery of man, which even today appears in those women who sacrifice their entire lives to nurse and care for subnormal offspring who cannot even speak and hardly understand! Strangely enough, it is the smallest, the most helpless, the most sickly which find shelter and protection. This is a power wise men have not bothered to investigate: it is an elusive power; it is furtive; it escapes. Perhaps it is the ultimate ground of Being, a "transcendence," which the philosophers, busy with more sublime matters, have neglected. But there, in that rocky navel of our globe, in the hidden, winding valley a female, fearful but defiant, protects her seven-month offspring. Should she be

discovered they would both be killed. Extreme weakness and tenderness are united and fused. As in love, man and woman are also united. A mystery emerges from this fusion. It does not move forward but backward; not toward the strongest but toward the weakest; not toward progress but toward regression. But from this return to what hardly seems viable, from that fusion of tenderness and human fragility, man is born.

Acurrucada en uno de esos rincones, lejos de las tribus de antropoides batalladores, una madre se empeña en hacer prosperar a su vástago, que en lenguaje humano llamaríamos hoy supersietemesino. El hombre ha nacido como sietemesino, como ser abortivo, imperfecto, utilizando ese margen de viabilidad que permite, con un poco de suerte y de cuidados, que no perezca lo que ha nacido anormal. La anormalidad de este extraño australopiteco residía en su extrema prematureidad. Millones de ellos fueron, probablemente, exterminados por las circunstancias, el clima hostil o los propios padres, irritados de haber procreado hijos biológicamente indigentes. Pero ¿por qué razón dentro de lo que se ha denominado—naturalmente, por el hombre—"dura ley de la selva" aparece otra ley, no menos importante, conforme a la cual cuánto más inválido e indefenso es un ser vivo, más ternura suscita, más deseo hay de conservar su vida? ¡Arcaico misterio del ser humano, que todavía hoy muestra su vigencia en esas mujeres que sacrifican toda su vida a la tutela de un subnormal que ni siquiera habla y que apenas comprende! Lo más pequeño, lo más inválido, lo más enfermo, encuentra, de manera extraña, un complemento, una correspondencia, algo que lo protege y ampara. Es una fuerza que los sabios no se han dignado investigar; que se esconde, furtiva; que se escabulle. Quizás un constituyente último del Ser, un "trascendente", en el que tampoco los filósofos han parado mientes, ocupados en menesteres más sublimes. Y, sin embargo, ahí, en ese ombligo rocoso del mundo, en los recovecos escondidos de un valle, una hembra, a la vez brava y temerosa, defiende y protege su vástago prematuro, sietemesino. Si la descubriesen, les matarían a los dos. Invalidez extrema y su correspondencia, la ternura, se funden y mezclan. Como en el amor, hombre y mujer también se funden. Un misterio nace de esta fusión. Que no parece llevar hacia adelante, sino hacia atrás; no hacia lo más fuerte, sino hacia lo más débil; no hacia el progreso, sino hacia la regresión. Mas de este retorno a lo que no parece viable, de esa fusión de la ternura y de la fragilidad va a nacer el hombre.[46]

The purely scientific content of this passage is soon absorbed by lyrical speculation and finally transformed into an esthetic emotion with a series of images thematically related to a central notion: the birth of man.

In the very first lines Rof circumvents the traditional notion of the evolutionary process as a survival of the fittest; he conceives of it rather as a precarious transition from a state of utter helplessness and near extinction to a miraculous survival made possible by a mother's tenderness. The confounding of past and present concentrates the experience of hominization—a struggle for survival over almost insurmountable obstacles in a span of millennia—in an eternal present. That is, each act of tenderness is a recapitulation of that initial state of helplessness and vulnerability which constitutes man's cosmic drama and paradoxically, mysteriously and wonderously molds the human spirit. Rof also suggests that the process of hominization is a passage from darkness to light. The image of man emerging from the cavernous, winding valleys of pre-history is often invoked. Thus, he speaks of "the mysterious night of the millennia" and of "a marvelous and mysterious concentration of tenderness" which through the centuries has made human existence possible. Human tenderness, then, rather than the struggle for existence, is that dark mysterious force buried in our archaic past which is paradoxically linked to the light which illuminates the ground of Being.

> But the ultimate secret of tenderness can be revealed to us only in that stirring moment when we are engulfed by it and experience that flowering of Being which springs from it. At this privileged moment man opens and expands as if he were guarding and awaiting the light of the Logos.
>
> Pero el último secreto de la ternura no podrá revelarse, probablemente, más que en ese conmovedor momento en que pudiéramos volver a estar dentro de ella en esa eclosión del Ser que nace bajo su tutela y en el que el hombre se abre o expande como alguien que, a la vez, guarda y aguarda la luz del Logos.[47]

Like Pascal, Rof conceives of man as a reed, a creature whose weakness is linked to his grandeur and for whom existence is a continual risk. In fact, the entire drama of evolution reveals the insurmountable risks of hominization: the threat of extinction, abandonment, violence, madness and death. Precisely because of this vulnerability of the species, Rof feels that any anthropology that does not stand in awe and reverence before the *tremendum* or *daenos* of man's origins is vitiated at its roots. For to recognize the fragility of existence and the mystery of our origins is the beginning of wisdom.

## The Function of the Image

A close look at Rof's poetic reconstruction of the "birth of man," reproduced above, reveals how an image can substitute for an idea and become an implicit form of argument. The author's thesis is that a mother's tenderness and care and not "the law of the jungle" account for the survival of man. In the quoted passage, the image of a mother and child huddled in a prehistoric cave confronting a forbidding environment becomes an implicit argument for the miraculous survival of civilization. We have here what Kenneth Burke has called the "imaginal equivalents of ideas."[48] These are not images which correspond to specific sense data but to concepts which transcend the empirical dimension of inquiry and representation and point to an intangible, invisible idea. As such, the imaginal equivalent of "mother" is more than the specific and particular idea of a woman or even an exact concept for tenderness and care. The image of the mother does not correspond to something; rather, it becomes an *image of identification* which provokes a cluster of emotions associated with care and protection. Rof's image, therefore, becomes an implicit argument for the importance of tenderness in the origins of civilization. In fact, the image of the mother represents the guiding principle of Rof's anthropology. Just as symbolic personification transforms cultural conflict into myth, so the imaginal equivalent transforms a *definite* idea into an *infinite*, intemporal dimension of experience.

*Conclusion*

We have seen that Rof's ultimate objective has been to preserve the human and divine family within the present structure of society. His work is, therefore, a defense of the basic values of the Judeo-Christian tradition.

Rof's use of myth to dramatize the human condition in an age of technology and unbelief is effective, but his approach to the problem of atheism is dated and unconvincing. The conservative religious humanism of men like Rof and Laín is the final expression of a line of thought made prominent by Marcelino Menéndez Pelayo at the turn of the century. It is an attempt to incorporate selectively the import of modern science and philosophy into traditional Catholic values. Like their predecessor, Rof and Laín are unwilling to recognize the full implications of secularization. In post Civil-War Spain, it was the philosophy of Zubiri that provided the Catholic intellectuals (namely Rof, Laín, Marías) with an orthodox answer to atheism. Now there is nothing wrong in invoking the ideas of Zubiri so long as they are seen in perspective: as solutions which are limited and must be superseded. But it is no exaggeration to say that Zubiri's classic essay "En

torno al problema de Dios" (1944) has, at least on religious issues, im-
mobilized the critical faculties of the Catholic segment of the gener-
ation of '36 which considers the text an ultimate indisputable state-
ment on contemporary theology. It has become a ritual among this
group to recite Zubiri's theory of *religación* at the conclusion of every
polemic against atheism. This inability or unwillingness to criticize
or go beyond Zubiri is perhaps the strongest criticism that can be
levelled at Rof and his group.

Rof's use of Segismundo as a symbolic personification of a root-
less and atheistic existence is also questionable. Here the author gives
unwitting testimony to his own theory that "we see through our blind-
ness." One critic has argued, for example, that Segismundo can be
considered a spokesman for values associated with a matriarchal so-
ciety.[49] In defying the superstitious and hyper-rationalistic attitude
of the king, Segismundo also rebels against an execessively demand-
ing and authoritarian father, the kind of figure Rof himself has iden-
tified with a tyrannical super-ego and with a caricature of the true
father. Not only does Segismundo rebel against traditional authority
(which at the end of the play he partially incorporates); he also repre-
sents qualities usually associated with feminine dispositions: spon-
taneity, passion, and a romantic revolutionary attitude. If Segismun-
do is *only* a symbol of atheism, could it be that Rof is guilty of the
very same kind of reductionism he attributes to Freud? Does Rof too
repress the feminine component in his character and is he blind to his
excessive identification with king Basilio?

# *Part Two:*

# *Socialist Humanism*

Is there not, first of all, a certain fraudulence in this word *human* which is always being thrown in our faces? If it is not a word quite devoid of meaning, what meaning does it really have?

Alain Robbe-Grillet, *For a New Novel*

# IV. THE NEW HUMANISM

## 1. Enrique Tierno Galván: Reality, Control, Happiness

In an essay on the political ideas of Dostoyevsky, Tierno credits the Russian novelist (and Kierkegaard) with having detected and announced the leap in Western consciousness from a concern for and an adaptability to the world (*ocupación*), to self-concern and inadaptability (*preocupación*). In our own time when introspection and self-analysis have acquired metaphysical status we can recognize in Dostoyevsky a prophet of modern sensibility. Now this penchant for self-concern, observes Tierno, manifests itself as an "unsatisfied intelligence," which is not to be confused with Hegel's unhappy consciousness nor with a psychological state or an epistemological problem. The unsatisfied intelligence is not an unsatisfied curiosity, but an intelligence which knows, comprehends but does not *understand*. And Dostoyevsky, for all his talent and vision, was unable to understand (*entender*) the social reality of his time. The possibility of understanding one's times as distinct from knowing (*conocer*) or comprehending (*comprender*) some or many of its cultural manifestations can come about only as the result of the social adaptability (*adecuación*) of intelligence. Understanding, then, is the faculty of intelligence which can be activated only by "a process of discontinuous adaptation to a *total* meaning of things" (DET 154). By total Tierno does not mean metaphysical or thorough knowledge but an "absolute intuitive compenetration with the object of understanding."

Tierno's semantic distinctions may appear baffling at first. In a sense the conceptual play on the meaning of knowledge—to know and comprehend, but not understand—strikes us as an inversion of the Biblical paradox of "They shall look. . .and not see. . . .Listen and not hear," so that inwardness is equivalent to illusion, or imperfect knowledge, whereas social sensibility is the way to true understanding. At any rate, toward the end of the essay Tierno makes this surprising statement: "Literary genius is for the most part a lack of understanding and Dostoyevsky appears to us as an exceptional case of social inadaptability." (DET 155)

Whereas the function of scientific demonstration is to explain and of philosophy to convince, that of literature is to seduce. The process of seduction is accomplished through the art of invention and narration, that is, by the substitution of an imaginary world for a concrete and real situation. The effectiveness of seduction depends not only on narrative skill but on the degree of withdrawal from concrete reality. Tierno has no objections to literature per se; he does not question the novelist's right to practice his craft or to indulge his fantasy. What he is pointing to is the unreliability of literature with philosophical pretensions and above all, to the degradation of a philosophy which resorts to literary techniques. Thus, metaphysics and existential analysis both betray an ignorance of the real world and share with literature the belief that words, not facts, constitute reality. The metaphysical view of reality resembles that of the novel in that for both the world becomes an object of absolute knowledge. In a novel we know all that has or could have happened. "Each novel is a world that has no more possibilities than those that have been created" (DET 275). Likewise in existential philosophy we find, like in a fictional situation, a pretension to knowing completely and totally the inner life of the individual. In short, "reality can be described literarily only insofar as it is invented" (DET 284); but the task of philosophy is not invention but the systematic explanation and critique of our immediate relation to reality. The philosophers who cannot convince will attempt to seduce, says Tierno, and they usually happen to be counterrevolutionaries. They are the talented individuals who do not understand because they are not adapted to the world. (DET 162)

Tierno's mission is to educate our social intelligence. The first step toward this goal is the destruction of the traditional assumptions of Western humanism, which include the need for a metaphysical view of reality and the exercise of subjectivism. Tierno states his purpose in the following manner:

> These reflections are in a way a modest contribution to the struggle against subjectivism. I believe. . .that subjectivism is the greatest obstacle to material and spiritual happiness. . . . By subjectivism, I mean a psychic space from which we oppose the world. The reduct of my egoism, my generosity, my pleasures and my grudges. It is the content of this "my" which has to change in meaning. We must adapt to the world in an absolute way, so that the consciousness of this adjust-

ment will replace subjectivism. . . .We would have to, in a way, go back to the pre-Socratics. The adjustment to the world, even when the world is hostile. In this sense philosophy becomes a therapeutic.

> Estas reflexiones no son, en cierto sentido, sino una contribución modesta a la lucha contra la intimidad. Yo creo. . .que la intimidad es el obstáculo mayor para obtener la felicidad material y espiritual. . . . La intimidad entendida como "espacio psíquico" desde el que nos oponemos al mundo. El reducto de mi egoísmo, mi generosidad, mis placeres y mis rencores. El sentido de este "mi" es el que tiene que cambiar. Tenemos que ajustar de modo absoluto con el mundo, de modo que la conciencia de este ajuste substituya a la intimidad. . . .Tendríamos que reencontrarnos con los presocráticos. El ajuste con el mundo incluso cuando el mundo es hostil. En este sentido la filosofía se convierte en terapéutica. (RR 159)

Reference to the pre-Socratics suggests that the mentality Tierno impugns is not confined in its expression to the obsessive self-analysis of a Kierkegaard or Dostoyevsky but includes an intellectual attitude of a broader spectrum known as humanism. In one of his earliest essays, Tierno reminds us that Socrates, from a social perspective, was not a truly educated man because he did not "respect with submission the world of objects for what they are" (DET 20). In fact, one of Tierno's basic objections to Greek thought, specifically the Platonic tradition, is its distrust of appearances and consequent predilection for metaphysics. There are other convictions of humanism which the author finds incompatible with social awareness; these are: 1) The belief that intelligence is superior to capacity (i.e. theory over praxis); 2) The belief that intelligence is unconditioned, hence, the humanist's negation of concrete reality and his identification of the intellect with a sensibility toward an esthetic understanding of the world; 3) A belief in the fundamental unity of past and present (theory of continuity), which often translates into an anti-revolutionary posture, and 4) The belief in ethical compatibility for both rich and poor. The theory of compatibility is for Tierno a basic assumption of traditional humanism. In practice, this means that in the realm of appearances constructed by an intelligence oblivious to social inequality it is easy to decree an ethic valid for both rich and poor and to practice tolerance. In sum, the two main objections to humanism are that it falsifies reality and that it is immoral.[1] Traditional humanism, based on the evolution of abstract notions, is not essential knowledge because its categories evolve according to self-determined principles and not as a result of social praxis. A true humanism must begin, for Tierno, with a sound social epistemology which will now be discussed.

## 2. Reality as Result

*La realidad como resultado* (1959) is a remarkably lucid treatise of some two hundred aphorisms on social epistemology written in the spirit of Francis Bacon's *Novum Organum* and Wittgenstein's *Tractatus*. This last work had a considerable influence on our subject's intellectual development. Tierno's aphoristic style stands out from the prolix, rambling, and digressive essays of some of his contemporaries. From the outset he states that the task of philosophy is to ask the right questions. Most "intellectuals," conditioned by a metaphysical training and alien to social reality, are falsifying both a theory of action and a method for transforming the world by engaging in endless psychological dissertations, exercises in self-analysis and a priori explanations of the meaning of history. What is the unifying principle of all reality? or What is its ultimate meaning and purpose? are not the right questions at this time. The right questions can only be directed at *what men have done.*

Reality for Tierno is the totality of culture. Culture is the result of men's deeds; thus reality is *result.* Reality is also *coactual;* that is, cultural phenomena are before me and I before them. But there are levels of coactuality and not all of them can be verified, although statements can be made about them. People, objects, ideas, planets, works of art, God, past, present, etc., are all coactual and therefore real. Reality, of course, is controlled ultimately by language, which, as suggested before, can always make a statement within its own level (systems of reference) of coactuality but cannot verify all these levels. In other words, some levels of coactuality have only syntactical validity (e.g. "being is") and are unverifiable propositions, whereas other levels of coactuality can be verified by evidence, instruments or logic.

Syntactical, linguistic propositions can be esthetically sound and morally edifying but they cannot be verified. Tierno is aware, of course, that there are such concerns as a search for God, the quest for beauty, etc., and that statements about them at the level of emotional coactuality are sincere, deeply felt and personally consequent. But since the author's concern is only with "what men have done" and what they can do under certain conditions, the best that can be said about such statements is that they are realities whose presence in the world is verifiable—but *only in the world.* Intellectually they are false linguistic propositions of worldly realities (coactualities). Thus, one can deny the possibility of proving God's existence and still feel deeply and genuinely religious. Again, that the moon is a heavenly body is a product of culture; it is a result of observation, study and feeling; the moon is what the species has done with it. But to ask who put the moon there is otiose.

But why this insistence on the verification principle, which in addition to being a theory of dubious standing is hardly a revolutionary method of social change? The verification principle is for Tierno only a first and necessary step in his struggle against metaphysics and the groundwork for his operational theory. It is also, as we shall see below, a tactic by which he suggests and encourages social change in a language ostensibly free from political connotations.

But to return to *Reality as Result*, it should be pointed out that the principal error Tierno attributes to the metaphysical mentality is the supposition that there is a fundamental unity to all levels of co-actuality and that signs pertaining to the psycho-physical level can be transposed to signify ultimate reality. Heidegger is a case in point in that he is not content to use anxiety as a neuro-physiological state; rather, the concept is extended to a metaphysical dimension and linked with the notion of nothingness as the source of being. For Tierno this is an illegitimate transposition from one plane of coactuality to another. A further instance of unwarranted linguistic transpositions pertains to the notion of death. The idea of death is a distinctly human phenomenon; therefore, insofar as the consciousness of death is a result of culture it is legitimate to ask what is death. But to posit the facticity of death as the ground of metaphysical speculation is untenable because "all metaphysical speculation construed on the facticity of death is esthetic invention" (RR 158). Now of course Tierno is fully aware that "esthetic invention" is the very heart of a genuine critical spirit, since most of his essays in the history of ideas and explorations into cultural topics are "esthetic" essays. The point he is trying to make here is that the esthetic attitude must recognize its limitations and renounce its ontological ambitions.

As a sociologist Tierno believes that "the humanist should be at the service of a science which transforms nature in accordance with those disciplines whose structure is experimental verification."[2] This, of course, is total empiricism, but it is Tierno's belief that the first step toward political transformation in a semideveloped country like Spain is the acceleration of economic development and the creation of an essentially consumer-oriented economy, which whould be intelligently and efficiently engineered by specialists, experts and professionals, all working for humane social goals. Tierno's thesis was and partially still is that economic growth, technological development and the formation of a middle class would necessarily bring about political change, thereby making revolution obsolete. The role of socialist opposition in this context is to determine the direction and structure of that inevitable change. If Spain becomes a nation of chemists, physicists and sociologists instead of politicians, lawyers, and non-practicing doctors then the present government will collapse under the weight of its own contradictions based on the abysmal inadequacy of the present political system to sustain the new economy.[3]

The "positive" (and optimistic) attitude is a conscious attempt at philosophical modesty and a much-needed antidote to an extravagant propensity among Spanish thinkers to confuse science with literature. In neopositivism Tierno found the precise, neutral language necessary for an effective operational sociology, a method free from metaphysical deformation and a corrective to the tenacious tyranny of the literary mentality in contemporary Spanish philosophy.[4]

Although in his esthetic essays Tierno has been sharp and consistent in his moral critique of Spanish society, he has, until recently, given little systematic thought to the ideological context of his sociology. Of revolution, he said in 1966 that it can no longer serve as a model for change in developed and semideveloped countries. Tierno does recognize in Marx the origins of modern sociology, but until 1969 there is no systematic exposition of such key terms as "dialectical reason," "praxis," and "revolution." In his theory for a social epistemology, written in 1966 with the title *Conocimiento y ciencias sociales*, Tierno absorbs the Marxist notion of praxis into his operational theory. "Generally, it can be said that neopositivism. . .has dispossessed Marxist theory of its metaphysical residues" (CCS 228). Thus, rather than risk metaphysical implications with terms like "dialectic," Tierno speaks of "operationalism" which is "the reduction of metaphysics to a theory of action. . . .For sociology to be operational it must accept the premise that the structure of all action defines the meaning of reality, and consequently that sociology is the only truly generalized theory of systems of human activity" (CCS 229).

In his latest work, however, Tierno has detected the possibility of ominous social consequences if operational reason is not coordinated with dialectical intelligence. In *Razón mecánica y razón dialéctica* (1969) he writes that "the extension of 'mechanical mentality'. . .does not satisfy, at least within the capitalist system, the aspirations of a great majority of the species" (RM 242). In other words, there is awareness on Tierno's part that an applied sociology cannot remain within the neutral confines of the empirical attitude but must be supported and complemented by a critical, negative thought. Therefore, "dialectical intelligence," which for centuries has served what Tierno calls the "esthetic mentality," must be incorporated into the positive methodology of social engineering if coexistence is to have a truly human dimension.

Tierno distinguishes dialectical reason from dialectical intelligence. Dialectical reason is the analysis of the transformational processes that occur when the techniques of the scientific method (mechanical reason) are applied. Dialectical intelligence, on the other hand, is synonymous with politics and ethics within the framework of a revolutionary ideology. Tierno mistrusts the term dialectic in the Marxist sense when it carries metaphysical connotations and prefers the neopositive expression "operational" which assumes that the structure of all action defines the meaning of reality. Thus, whereas neopositivism is a scientific tool, a calculus of objective reality, dialectical intelligence is the critical consciousness directed toward the transformation of the social order. The first provides the theoretical basis of mechanical reason: operational techniques necessary for the scientific control of reality. The second becomes the philosopher's critical posture and moral imperative to coordinate reflection with action and end human exploitation. The acceptance and utilization of mechanical reason implies that "reality" is a world of closed possibilities in which we are included and that each possibility predetermines the other. Dialectic means, for Tierno, the consciousness of the possibilities of dominating, controlling the possibilities offered by mechanical reason, and accelerating its process. In short, mechanical reason is a scientific idea and dialectic is a political idea. The supreme moral exigency of our time, the need to end human exploitation, can come about only with the integration of a mechanical mentality with dialectical intelligence. Politics, ethics and dialectics coincide.

In summary: Tierno Galván's explicit philosophical objective is to substitute the metaphysical concerns prevalent in contemporary Spanish thought with a positive critical attitude and to replace subjectivism, self-analysis (*intimismo*), and abstract discourse (*esteticismo*) with a scientific and dialectical vocabulary capable of describing the structure of social reality. Implicit in Tierno's approach is an effort to draw attention to the political problems of his country and provide a theory of action consonant with socialist values. The author's disdain for metaphysics and his recourse to a positive order of meaning is an intellectual response to the poverty of systematic social thought and a moral response to the political status quo in present day Spain.

## 3. A Rhetoric of Anti-Humanism

Tierno's rhetoric consists essentially in the inversion of the traditional philosophical and moral categories associated with classical humanism: beauty, harmony, interior peace, and concord are humanistic themes seen from an esthetic perspective. To this attitude Tierno opposes the primacy of utility and efficiency. The objective of traditional humanists "is to admire and be admired, a state of consciousness which depends on the suspension of any resistance" (CCS 210). But the theme of our time, avers the author, is not self-admiration but utility. The new humanism is therefore an antihumanism; this means that "only the useful is beautiful and that the content of beauty is not admiration but well-being (*bienestar*)" (*ibid.*). As a result, terms which have become abhorrent to classical humanism, such as control, verifiability, material well-being, planning, operational, acquire in the work of Tierno a morally positive meaning.

It would hardly be worth analyzing the rhetoric of a writer who had merely substituted one order of meaning for another, especially when his principal aim is to compose a formal system in a highly specialized scientific language. What is of interest in the work of Tierno is not his attempt to formulate a new social epistemology but the language of negation, that is, his critique of traditional humanism. In this facet of his work one encounters an often shocking combination of ideas whose critical and corrosive force jolts the reader from a familiar pattern of conceptual association forcing him to reevaluate a habitual and standard perception of culture. In this sense Tierno's figures of thought offer a semantic richness worth exploring. His aphorisms, like those of Nietzsche, challenge the sensibility to explore beyond the confines of accepted intellectual canons. But before offering specific examples of Tierno's creative negation, the cultural category *esthetic* should be explained in its function as a rhetorical figure.

*The esthetic sensibility*

Tierno calls "esthetic" a number of intellectual attitudes which he feels are evasive, immoral and illusory, or theories which falsify reality. But in addition to a pejorative meaning esthetic also has a neutral or even a positive connotation when it is an expression of *totalization*. Thus the formulation of general laws or unifying principles which characterize a period is an example of totalization: an undifferentiated, emotional response to the reality of culture, which does not have epistemological status. The philosophy of Hegel and the theology of Teilhard de Chardin are typical examples of the esthetic sensibility expressed in totalization. In fact, it is the task of religion, observes Tierno, to express the spirit of the times as a process of totalization. Should religion fail in this task its function becomes nothing more than arbitrary speculation. The term esthetic, then, is a total undifferentiated apprehension of all that is coactual. In this sense it stands in opposition to science, which adopts a differentiated and specific attitude. What follows is a list of contexts in which the term esthetic appears.

A. The view of Spanish history is too often *esthetic,* by which Tierno means that is mystified. Thus the consequences of the Civil War of 1936 have been *esthetic* in that the exiles have perpetuated a myth of Spain based on the works of three of its greatest mythologizers: Unamuno, Lorca and Ortega (A 315). The notion of a "Spannish character" or of an "essence of Spain" is an esthetic view of history. Spain, in fact, is the esthetic nation par excellance. In most European countries during the Renaissance the esthetic view of the world substituted for the faltering cultural function of religion, but in Spain the early and sophisticated development of the novel is an esthetic compensation and substitute for "a curiosity about the world and the desire to possess it, the bourgeois, mercantile view of society, and the modern notion of freedom" (DET 280). In Holland, where commercial activity was unusually intense, the novel developed much later. In Spain, where the commercial mentality was deprecated, the novel appears in all its modernity as a substitute for the incapacity to interpret and adapt to the bourgeois world. (DET 281)

B. "Esthetic humanism, the only humanism we have known, is essentially immoral" (RM 242). "Esthetics and religion appear as if they were fundamentally eroticism without desire" (RR 138). "The social group with a privileged economic status tends to have an esthetic concept of the world" (RR 170). "Tradition: a heritage of acritical attitudes. Tradition is a word with a preferably esthetic meaning" (RR 160). Romanticism and psychoanalysis are esthetic attitudes. Esthetic knowledge says nothing about the nature of that which it has apprehended, "it only reveals its meaning in relation to specific states of consciousness" (CCS 21). "Metaphysics has its own problems, it aspires to be a leading discipline and pretends to situate itself on a speculative plane superior to that of science." In other words, it becomes an esthetic discipline which will be preferred by the bourgeois.

## Literary terminology as rhetoric

Consistent with his negative view of the esthetic attitude, Tierno also employs literary terminology to distinguish genuine thought from pseudo-philosophy.

A. In the work of Heidegger Tierno notes a *literary* intention to give a metaphysical meaning to words that can only reflect an emotional state, e.g., anxiety. All this, says Tierno, is nothing but a *literary* game, "precisely by literature we understand existence as a plot *(argumento),* that is, the imaginary causal process of intentions, conducts and connections." (RR 118)

B. Philosophy has not only become an academic discipline, but has attempted to express itself as a style of life, that is, "as a turning into literature *(literaturización)* the basis of human conduct" (A 249). "The novel is a process in which the world becomes the object of absolute knowledge." (DET 275)

C. We are living, reasons Tierno, in a period of simultaneity (of experience), the fragmentation and atomization of knowledge and the loss of faith in a linear concept of history and in the theory of progress. A society that still believes in progress is a "genetic culture" with a "literary view of history" by which Tierno means that it still subscribes firmly to the idea of the transmission of values (tradition). The *literary* view of history should be reduced or transformed into a *poetic* view of reality which coincides with the experience of simultaneity and fragmentation. Genetic societies are underdeveloped nations, while the experience of simultaneity corresponds to material well-being *(bienestar).* The mentality proper to simultaneity is that of admission or recognition *(admisión).* "All that is happening around us, our very lives, is recognized without much tension or criticism. The contemplation of reality as a recognized fact, as something that carries within itself its genesis and justification, characterizes modern Western man. A *dramatic* recognition, that is, a non-recognition, characterizes existentialism and other old attitudes" (TM 168). The history of science, claims Tierno, has falsely construed the idea that inventions and the creative spirit follow a rigorous, successive pattern. "On the contrary, it so happens that the great discoveries do not have antecedents. To explain them as a causal process is to give them a *plot,* that is, grant them a *literary structure.*" (TM 173)

D. Plato's fusion of literaure and philosophy in his *Dialogues* established the basis of dialectical intelligence, which is interchangeable with *literary intelligence.* Dialogue is the essence of humanism: it incorporates life into the process of reason within the structure of coexistence. The structure of the dialogue is the human structure of the logos, which coincides with being. "Dialectical intelligence, that is, a *literary plot (argumento literario)* able to comprise the totality of process, begins with humanism and its best means of expression is the *dialogue*" (RM 52). When dialectic is divorced from dialogue, from *literature,* it becomes mechanical reason or science. Scientific exposition is incompatible with the structure of dialogue. Today, dialectical intelligence cannot be founded on dialogue, but must be at the service of mechanical reason through praxis. "A proletariat whose politics would consist in dialogue strikes us as a monstrosity. . . .The structure of praxis insofar as it is process has some formal resemblance to the structure of dialogue, but neither dialogue nor dialectical intelligence can express the world today as it is, only the way it has been, because today the notion of praxis is defined essentially by the concept of revolution." (RM 255)

*Definitions and Allusions*

In addition to terms such as esthetic and literary there are other key concepts in Tierno's critique of culture which either define or allude to a particular social phenomenon. Definitions pertain to culture in general, whereas the allusions are almost exclusively directed at post-Civil War Spain.

Tierno has referred to post-Civil War Spain as a culture of *hibernation,* that is, a soporific climate of artistic inactivity and intellectual stupor in which the functions that sustain culture are so lethargic and debilitated that existence goes on purely at the biological level. It is a state of affairs in which there isn't even an esthetic substitution for the volatile or weak sectors of culture. In the same collection of essays Tierno makes a subtle connection between Spanish politics during the Counter-Reformation and Franco's regime: he speaks of social immobility and intellectual stagnation in terms of cultural "Byzantinism." But the biological notion of hibernation becomes an extended metaphor when Tierno modulates its meaning to cover ironically the proverbial vitality of the Spanish people. When associated with Spain the word vitality has become synonymous with a spontaneity and exuberance of a people whose style of life is markedly different from—and to many Spanish intellectuals superior to—the rest of European nations, who are more inclined to philosophical speculation and science than artistic expression. But Tierno associates vitality in the culture of hibernation with a sub-human existence more proper to sheep than men. This seems to be a veiled reply to Ortega y Gasset's remark upon his return to Spain after World War II that he had faith in Spain's cultural recovery because of its almost "indecent intellectual vitality" and to Julián Marías' remark that "Spain's intellectual vitality is such that she can even permit herself to fall into error."[5] What Marías calls intellectual vitality is for Tierno existence at the trophic level, a form of inhumanity *(inhumanismo)* nurtured by a culture of hibernation. One can speak of the vitality of sheep, he notes, but this is not a vitality proper to a community of men. On the contrary, "the supreme example of inhumanity is the sheepfold." That the culture of hibernation is not a self-imposed condition should be obvious to anyone familiar with post-Civil War Spanish history, but the causal relationship between culture and politics is barely implied here, for reasons that are obvious. However, in an essay on the psychology of conspiracy, written six years later, Tierno asserts in an ostensibly impartial language that tyranny rests on a moral corruption that reduces men to the condition of animals. But Tierno also cautions those living under the tyranny of passivity and cowardice. In his essay on the culture of hibernation, in which he made explicit reference to Spain, he only suggested the need for a literature of protest to awaken the Spaniards from their slumber. In the *Anatomía de la conspiración* the subject of political oppression is treated in its universal dimension but the allusion to Spain is frequent. Here Tierno states openly that "to be fearful of political power is immoral."[6]

## The language of provocation

Following the distinction in traditional rhetoric between figures of word and figures of thought one can accordingly speak of verbal and conceptual provocation, always keeping in mind, of course, that they are sometimes inseparable. For the sake of analysis I have isolated particular fragments of provocative language from its total conceptual context in much the same way as one could isolate a metaphor from an analogy or an analogy from an allegory.

By provocation I mean the power of language to effect a disruption of a normal pattern of conceptual association which permits the reader to perceive an idea in a new context and which at the same time elicits a response of affirmation or negation. When Nietzsche, for example, refers to God as a spider, or when he calls beliefs more dangerous than lies, he is expressing in a provocative combination of words an intuitive subversion of values. Intuitive because the insight is pointed and condensed; it is not a systematic, logical-discursive subversion (i.e. Kant's *Critique of Pure Reason*).

The bases of Tierno's provocative styles are the numerous antinomies and antitheses which abound in his prose. Thus he speaks of "*fecund promiscuity* of Science and Philosophy" (A 91); or he characterizes liberal protest as "the *demagogy of trust*" (HR 95) or again in speaking of the way the mass media have institutionalized violence and offer it as a substitute for literature, he refers to the phenomenon as a "cerebral *didactic violence*" (HR 108). There are other pregnant, provocative statements that disrupt a habitual pattern of conceptual association pertaining to cultural values. Thus: "the *trivial* is *destiny*" (DET 327); "*Philosophy* should be a *vulgar discipline*" (A 285); "The scientific *control* of human relations will lead to *happiness*" (DCP 31), which must be understood dialectically (see below); "*Socrates was not an educated man*" (DET 20); "esthetics and religion are like *eroticism without desire*" (RR 138); "If novels had been written by impresarios, Western man would have been saner." (DCP 18)

The ultimate function of the antinomical definitions and antitheses is to undermine the humanistic disposition to admire (*admiratio*) with a corrosive disassociation of concepts. Broadening the context of provocative language we can see this same technique at work with figures of thought aimed at the subversion of some of the topics of classical humanism.

*The anti-topics*

The humanistic topic of the wonder that is man is perhaps best expressed in Michelangelo. At least so believes Laín, who in an essay discussed in a previous chapter finds in the majestic statues of David and Moses the most dramatic expression of the fulfillment of human vocation and destiny (both concepts, let us remember, form the core of Orteguian ethics). Tierno, on the other hand, sees in Michelangelo a vigorous expression of narcissism, adding derisively that in his figures "the rhetoric of greatness reaches laughable proportions" (A 54).

97

This rhetoric of greatness, continues Tierno, was made current by those Renaissance "comedians" obsessed with ideal beauty known as artists whose attitude manifests itself either as disdain or mere gesture (*gesticulación*) rather than human substance.

Anthropomorphism, the essence of humanism, is in Tierno's view a farcical and fraudulent exercise in egoism and self-deification because it is rooted in that *intimismo* and will to transcendence which distorts the true condition of man. A variation on the theme of the farcical aspect of humanism appears in the essay "Quality and Quantity." The humanists, we are told, are hunters of qualities which they consider independent of quantity. But today, the metaphysical status of quality is a myth: quality can no longer "impregnate" quantity, rather, it can only be an outgrowth of it, that is, of abundance. Our task, suggests Tierno, is to create new qualities on the basis of this inversion of categories. Now those who live according to self-sustained qualities in a world of quantity are *hypocrites* and *Tartuffes* (HR 38, 46) because they attempt to manipulate quantities without accepting them as genuine sources of quality. Like Moliere's protagonist they believe that the repetition of virtuous poses and gestures will have a cumulative effect and reveal them as truly virtuous. Eventually the the simulation is discovered: the insincerity of his relation to quantity is disclosed. This is the case of the humanist intellectual.

The intellectual, in the traditional sense, is also seen by Tierno as a clown: his inadaptability to the world inspires laughter as well as sadness, in fact, "humanisitic intelligence and sadness are inseparable" (DCP 7). It is a sadness that originates in the consciousness of an unjustified passivity before a need to change the world which the intellectual dramatizes with ritual self-mythification to placate his conscience. By mythification Tierno means a process of deceptive self-justification before an ideology and its institutions that the intellectual knows have no moral justification. In other words, self-mythification is a subjective falsification devised to maintain the status quo. The intellectual's ironic and clownish attitude is the manifestation of the gap between the self-mythologized view of the role of intelligence and genuine moral obligation. Praxis, notes Tierno, is philosophically speaking, the opposite of irony. (RM 255)

One must distinguish, however, as Tierno does not, between ironic distance, which is a specifically critical posture, and a foolhardy affirmation of values known to be objectively false. Both reveal the basic contradictions between personal aspiration and objective reality, but they differ in that the first attitude is devoid of identification with these aspirations, transforming them into despair, the absurd, in short into the tragic vision; whereas the intrinsic optimism (hope) of a humanism based on admiration, imitation, perfection and recovery of *essential* human values (e.g. contemporary Catholic humanism in Spain) is an ingenuous affirmation which attempts to suppress its own contradictions.

It was noted in a previous chapter that a frequent rhetorical device of conservative humanism was the cultivation of its own traditional topics: vocation, destiny, leisure, the family, anti-technology, harmony of politics and ethics, etc. In Tierno's view these topics acquire comical and even pathetic proportions because the personal psychology that sustains them is rooted in bad faith, in that willing ignorance of the world. Now a topic is normally validated by opinion, which makes it in a way an impersonal form of communication. Its impersonality is sustained by an implicit message or allusion which the public or group recognizes as true, or obvious. But Tierno has noted that there is a personal dimension to topical discourse in which "a stratum of consciousness denounces the artificiality of a stated topic by recognizing simultaneously its emptiness." This is particularly true in authoritarian societies where what we know as criticism is blunted or diverted by the restriction of discourse to fixed topics. Thus formulaic moral exhortations directed at a government whose indifference to reform may require political rather than moral solutions creates in many intellectuals a false happiness characterized by "tragic tension between the superficial and the profound" (DET 116). Here again we have this quasi-farcical, tragicomic contradiction between the intellectual and society. But the tension Tierno speaks of need not result necessarily, one would think, from a "willing ignorance of the world," but also perhaps from political impotence that consoles itself with moral criticism but is unable to enter the realm of action. Tierno, of course, has called this impotence a fear of power which to him is essentially immoral.

Perhaps the most discussed topic in the post-Civil War period was "the problem of Spain," the preoccupation with national essence and destiny derived from the conflicting cultural interpretations of the Spanish heritage among liberals and traditionalists, to which we should add such corollary topics as "the psychology of the Spanish people" and the "conflict between Spanish Catholicism and secularization." Now these were themes long exhausted by the generation of '98, yet they became a series of tediously prolonged polemics and quixotic exercises in *Volksgeist* analysis. When every country in

Europe has long ceased looking for its essence in favor of more urgent philosophical problems, Spain, complains Tierno, stubbornly and foolishly insists on maintaining a mythical view of itself which contradicts the most elementary realities of the modern world.

Tierno has attacked practically every topic in contemporary Spain, showing how it is connected to the process of mythification, that is, the subjective falsification resulting from an implicit recognition of the ineffectiveness of the ideology that is upheld. In his brief essay *Diderot como pretexto* (Diderot as a Pretext) he has shown how mythification increases in proportion to the weakening of the ideologies it attempts to justify. Thus, when someone has to keep affirming that he is a "good father" in spite of the fact that the family as an institution is in crisis, it is a sign that in fact the present function of the family is no longer a viable form of coexistence. Here we have a good example of how Tierno's critique of society brings him in direct opposition to the conservative humanism of Rof Carballo (ch. III) who has exploited perhaps more than anyone the topic of the family.

The main thrust of Rof's argument against Freud and some of his followers was that neither a critical ego nor a sound social pedagogy can replace the function of the father, who is an indestructible archetype and the indispensable image in the process of human development. Rof's ultimate motives were, of course, to insure the permanence of the human, and divine, family in the modern world. Tierno's point of view is different. "The family," he writes, "is the institution which has contributed most to the mythification of modern man" (DCP 25). The moral disintegration of the family in developed nations is but the erosion of the purely economic (*patrimonio*) structure of the institution of marriage. But once marriage ceases to be a means of perpetuating interests and is reduced precisely to what it is supposed to be, a bond based on affection, then its mythical dimension is revealed. Tierno is convinced that the family as we know it is an alienated form of interpersonal relationship with no genuine social function. At one point his reaction is quite strong:

> The great number of falsehoods nurtured by the mythification of the family group in our time is destructive even when seen from the standard moral ideology. Fidelity hardly exists any more, or else is maintained only through continuous repression. There is no deeply felt *love* for the children in the sense the mythologized individual uses the term. The love of offspring is the ingredient of mythification which contributes to obscure the fact that conjugal life is a painful obligation.

El conjunto de falsedades que nutre la mitologización de los miembros de la familia contemporánea es destructivo, incluso desde la ideología moral al uso. Apenas existe la fidelidad o se mantiene con represión psíquica. No existe el *amor* entrañable por los hijos en el sentido pleno que la personalidad mitologizada atribuye a la palabra. El amor por los hijos es el ingrediente de la mitologización que contribuye a oscurerecer el hecho de la vida conjugal como un deber penoso (DCP 27).

There is little doubt that Tierno would consider as a purely "esthetic" argument Rof Carballo's defense of the family based on man's gratitude for having been cared for and on the image of the father as a source of identity.

But Tierno's most obvious and pervasive "antitopic" is the idea of *trivialization*, which is aimed directly at the rhetorical admiration of the grandeur of man. The traditional humanist's earnest introspection and cultivation of leisure and solitude, his dedication to personal perfection and the fulfillment of a vocation and destiny, appear to Tierno as an anachronistic tragicomedy manifesting the contradiction between a highly individualistic anthropology and present social reality.

Trivialization is the present state of culture in which the important and the ordinary are experienced at the same level of intensity. In other words, culture is no longer dramatic. The trivialization of eroticism (its desublimation) and of political power (rejection of sacrifice) are both derived from modern man's loss of asceticism. Implicit in the process of trivialization is conformism and the desire for material well-being. Conformism, of course, is exactly the opposite of asceticism. The question Tierno asks then is "Once the process of trivialization comes to an end can conformism lose its negative elements and become the expression of a happy coexistence?" (DET 322). The duty of the intellectual would be to accept conformity as the most authentic mode of existence in our time. Hence Tierno's pointed statement that "the trivial is destiny." A tragedy without asceticism in which conformity itself is the essence of the tragic. In sum: "Conformity as well as trivialization are transitional, they point to a period without asceticism and without the emptiness and nostalgia for the ascetic: to the man of the future, free from an interior self (*intimidad*) for whom esthetics will be integrated into well-being" (DET 327).

*Style and Thought: The dialectical function of the essay*

It should be fairly clear by now that positivism (mechanical reason) has a dialectical function in Tierno's thought. The total affirmation of the scientific method is not a proclamation of scientism but a response to a historical moment in Spain which calls for the destruction of the categories of traditional humanism. Thus, while as a sociologist Tierno is a thorough neopositivist, he is also able to deny scientific mentality the status of an absolute value through the exercise of dialectical intelligence. Stated in his own words, it is "a matter of strengthening the results of mechanical reason with dialectical intelligence so that science itself can annul a scientific mentality" (RM 254). Science becomes an anti-humanism only to become the fertile ground of a new humanism. The primacy of man (anthropocentrism and anthropomorphism) is negated in the name of a more human society. Dialectical intelligence as a criticism of ideology is the express instrument of negation and affirmation: on the one hand it subverts the humanistic *Weltanschauung* by inverting its basic categories and values, on the other hand, it remains in the service of dialectical reason as an instrument of praxis.

If the conceptual instrument of negation is dialectical intelligence, its literary form is the essay. Theodor Adorno has suggested that the essay as a form implies a consciousness of "non-identity" which, in its critique of doctrine, ideology, or total and so-called "eternal" knowledge, establishes a partial, ephemeral, historical truth.[7] In other words, as the consciousness of a mediating function of partial knowledge, the essay is an expression of a non-truth in the form of negation (of the absolute) which thereby affirms an historical truth. Its non-truth is derived not only from its limited objectives and lack of method but from the fact that it is a culturally derived form.

But if the essay as a genre affirms the temporal and the particular against absolute and total knowledge, what accounts for the difference between such essayists as Laín, who perceive every cultural phenomenon *sub specie aeternitatis*, and the negative critique of Tierno? The obvious difference, of course, is philosophical but the formal difference, I submit, is rhetorical. A partial truth may be either associated with or subsumed to a model in which case it is only an accidental manifestation of an essence; or, as in the case of Tierno, the partial truth as the consciousness of "non-identity" (Adorno), is *dissociated* from all transcendental, total and absolute meaning.

It was observed above how linguistic antinomies and conceptual antitheses served the subversive function of breaking down a habitual association of ideas that Tierno felt were congenial to traditional humanism. In addition Tierno also employs the aphorism as a technique of dissociation. It is appropriate to mention here that Tierno's doctoral dissertation was a study of Tacitism in the political doctrines of the Spanish Golden Age.[8] The Tacitists were political theorists who wished to formulate a rigorous science of politics and divorce it from ethical and religious contingencies. The Tacitists were opposed in Spain because their doctrine was frequently associated with Machiavelli, who represented a threat to the temporal-religious unity of the Catholic monarchy. In their effort to dissociate the science of politics from ancillary, obstrusive disciplines the Tacitists resorted to the aphorism to emphasize rigor and precision of thought. Their method was to express in brief, pointed sentences a particular idea or circumstance which would give insight into the workings of political power. On the model of the Tacitists, Tierno employs the aphorism to dissociate what he considers essential knowledge from metaphysics, literature and "humanistic falsification." When considered dialectically, of course, Tierno's ultimate aim is to be both moral and political. Juan Marichal is correct, then, in referring to Tierno's style as "*neotacitismo*," or a response to the need in Spain to fuse effectively politics and ethics.[9]

The aphorism as a terse, compact and concentrated expression of thought gives ideas both contour and profundity, because it can emphasize, individualize and atomize a concept through spaced sequences. Tierno's two hundred aphorisms have a thematic unity but not what he would call a plot or a "literary progression." Essentially, the aphorism is for Tierno a formal tool of exact definition, economy of thought and intellectual rigor and precision. One can only appreciate this tendency in juxtaposition with the prolixity, ambiguity, evasion, cryptic style, and love of digression that characterizes much of post-Civil War Spanish thought. Above all, Tierno consciously avoids digression, of which he has this to say in one of his aphorisms: "There is nothing more opposed to the mentality of our time than digression (*divagación*). Digressive rambling is repugnant to the economy of effort that characterizes contemporary Western culture." (RR 116)

Tierno's use of the aphorism invites a comparison with Francis Bacon, whom he admired along with the rest of the British empirical tradition. Both employ the aphorism as a tool of epistemology, but where the object of inquiry for Bacon is nature, for Tierno it is culture and where in one case the enemy is scholasticism for the Spaniard it is metaphysics. But where the comparison is most appropriate is perhaps in their rejection of humanistic standards of philosophical expression. Bacon, like Tierno, deplores "men who hunt more after words than matter; more after choiceness of the phrase. . .and the varying and illustration of their words with tropes and figures than after the weight of matter, worth of subject. . ."[10] Or when in the *Novum Organum* he remarks that "men believe that their reason governs words; but it is also true that words react on the understanding; and this has rendered philosophy and the sciences sophistical and inactive."[11] Bacon, however, enjoyed the use of figurative language, and some of his most memorable insights are communicated with metaphors and similes, the very tropes whose excessive use he condemned. Tierno, on the other hand, is a literalist who avoids any form of transposition, perhaps because he is aware of the implicit subjectivity in metaphorical or analogical discourse. Tierno's chief linguistic weapon is, as we have seen, *dissociation through antithesis.*

Moving from the aphorism to the essay in general one finds in the writings of Tierno a total absence of the traditional *exordium* or preliminaries, which again reflects his quest for objectivity and economy. The exordium is normally used to make the reader (audience) well-disposed toward the author. In many cases it is used for apologetic reasons (affirmations of modesty, pretensions of ignorance, expressions of hypocritical humility). The exordium is perhaps that part of argumentation which is most *personal,* for it is a conscious attempt to qualify the speaker for his task of presenting the material at hand, and perhaps this is the reason why Tierno, in his effort to avoid any subjective contamination of content, avoids it. Every essay and book Tierno has written dispenses with the exordium.

## Tierno and Socialism

In addition to being a philosopher of praxis Tierno is a leading opposition figure in Franco's Spain, the principal theoretician of his own Social-Democratic party and certainly the most articulate spokesman for socialism in Spain. He has encouraged and participated in anti-regime protests which cost him, in 1965, the chair of political science at the University of Salamanca. Subsequently he has been subjected to frequent political harassment by the authorities.

It is no exaggeration to affirm that Tierno is the most capable and impressive philosopher in the history of Spanish non-utopian Socialism. He possesses an encyclopedic knowledge, a penetrating intellect and a lucid style. He may have been superseded by socialist thinkers before him in other qualities such as organizational abilities and political acumen, but Tierno is surely the master scientific theorist of social knowledge. There are at least three reasons for this: unlike his predecessors Tierno is thoroughly familiar with Marxism, has developed a more sophisticated and systematic social theory, and, what is most important in the context of this study, he is the first non-utopian socialist to have shed the last residues of personalist humanism.[12] A few words are needed to clarify these assertions.

Although Marx has been frequently invoked by Spanish socialists he has been often the victim of "humanistic reductionism" by theorists who found his anthropology and social goals appealing, but could hardly cope with the richness and complexity of Marxian thought. But, curiously enough, from the last quarter of the 19th century to 1936 it was the non-socialist, conservative thinkers such as Costa, Clarín, Unamuno and Ortega who not only understood Marx better than their socialist contemporaries but who were also the keenest critics of social reality.

If one were to look for Tierno's predecessor, Jaime Vera (1859-1918) would be a likely candidate, as well as possibly, in some ways, Núñez de Arenas (1886-1951). Like Tierno, Vera rejected the moral-ideological basis of social problems and sought in socialism a scientific, dialectical instrument for the transformation of society. Vera's *Informe a la Comisión de Reformas Sociales* (1884) is, if not in sophistication of method then at least in spirit, close to Tierno's sociological orientation. With Núñez de Arenas, founder of the socialist group *La Escuela Nueva* (1911), Tierno shares a respect for the verification principle and the need to integrate fully all the expressions of culture into society. What is particularly noteworthy of socialist thinkers such as Vera, Núñez de Arenas and later Fernando de los Ríos (1879-1949) and Julián Besteiro (1870-1940) is their ability to analyze specific social phenomena with a sound scientific methodology. One thinks of Núñez de Arenas' *Notas sobre el movimiento obrero* and de los Ríos' *El problema ferroviario español* as studies which define concrete, specific social issues in the context of national politics and broader historical forces.[13] But none of these thinkers can compare with Tierno in the depth and sophistication of social analysis nor in philosophical method.

But the greatest difference between Tierno and his predecessors is one of attitude toward that vague concept humanism, for unlike the socialist thinkers mentioned above Tierno is the first to have shed completely the last residues of a personalist or ethicist humanism. This implies a total break with 19th century reformist and regenerationist rhetoric, a rejection of the educational utopianism and moral ideology of the Krausists perpetuated by socialists such as F. de los Ríos and Julián Besteiro. In Tierno we have a categorical rejection of traditional ethical humanism. The following fragments, taken respectively from F. de los Ríos' *El sentido humanista del socialismo* (1926) and from Núñez's essay "El valor del hombre en la ideología marxista," published in the journal *España* (1918) represent a view of man and a mode of expression totally alien to Tierno's modern humanism:

> Socialism can refresh and spiritualize the soul. . . .Marxism has ceased to have contact with socialist humanism both in relation to its basis and to its ends.
>
> . . . . . . . . . . . . . . . . . . . . . . . . . . . . . . . . . . . . . . . . . . . . . . . . . . . . . .
>
> The Marxists have simplified man and have mutilated him, emphasizing only his material need and ignoring such ideal conflicts as that of religion and family. . . .Human sensibility simply doesn't count. . . . Socialism. . .presupposes the specific aptitude to nurture with a new human love all that is noble and spiritually great in civilization.
>
> *España* XL, junio, 1918, p. 4)

## Conclusion

Tierno Galván's critical essays are a reaction against what he terms a literary sensibility in Spanish thought, characterized by gesture instead of substance, invention in place of criticism, appreciation and admiration in favor of scientific discipline, and subjectivism instead of social consciousness. The result of this "estheticism" is personal and social myth which results in a falsification of reality. One myth Tierno is particularly eager to discredit is the notion, so widely disseminated by the generation of '98, that science and the Spanish character are incompatible. Everyone is familiar with Unamuno's contemptuous, "¡Que inventen ellos!" (Let them [Europeans] invent!). But already in Ganivet, the precursor of the generation of '98, we get the very essence of what Tierno calls the esthetic mentality. In one of the most "mythologized" versions of Spain, *Idearium español*, Ganivet has this to say about the Spanish character:

> A case in point is our turning away from the applied sciences; there is no way of establishing them in Spain, not even by converting our men of science into functionaries paid by the state. It's not that there are no men of science; there always have been and there still are; but when they are not of a mediocre intelligence they feel drawn to heights where Science denaturalizes itself and becomes mixed either with religion or art. Castelar wants to be a historian, and his studies

are transformed into epic songs; Echegaray, a mathematician and dramatist, handles numbers with a mastery and profound spiritualism of the Pythagoreans. . .

> A la vista está nuestro desvío de las ciencias de aplicación; no hay medio de hacerlas arraigar en España, ni aun convirtiendo a los hombres de ciencia en funcionarios retribuidos por el Estado. Y no es que no haya hombres de ciencia; los ha habido y los hay; pero cuando no son de inteligencia mediocre, se sienten arrastrados hacia las alturas donde la ciencia se desnaturaliza, combinándose ya con la religión, ya con el arte. Castelar quiere ser historiador, y sus estudios se le transforman en cantos épico-oratorios; Echegaray, matemático y dramaturgo, maneja los números con la maestría y profundo espiritualismo de los pitagóricos. . .

Whatever truth there may be in such a view of Spanish culture it is for Tierno no longer a realistic and responsible one. It is an attitude which only prolongs the confusion between philosophy and literature and perpetuates subjectivism. With uncommon directness and candor Tierno has made himself very clear on the issue of humanism:

> Generally, any type of book which explains the world as the dwelling of man has been written by people whose knowledge implied their own lack of consciousness of falsehood, especially if the book was written or interpreted in view of the exigencies of an industrial society. The intellectuals have constructed for us a symbolic universe which is falling apart; what we must do is hasten its collapse.

> En general cualquier clase de libro que explica al mundo como como lugar del hombre ha sido escrito por gentes cuyo conocimiento implicaba la penuria propia de la conciencia de la falsedad, particularmente si el libro se escribía o se interpretaba desde las exigencias de la sociedad industrial. Los intelectuales nos han construido un universo simbólico que se está cayendo, pero hay que ayudar a que se caiga más de prisa. (DCP 18)

Over a half century ago Ortega y Gasset wrote that if we write good literature, but we feel that we are also capable of science, our decision must be to opt unequivocally for the latter. Tierno feels that such a decision is yet to be taken, with seriousness, dedication and discipline.

# V. JOSE LUIS ARANGUREN AND THE ROLE OF THE MORALIST IN OUR TIME

Notwithstanding the frequent abuse of the category "transitional figure" in histories of literature, the term is in the case of J.L. Aranguren an appropriate and precise definition of his place in post-Civil War letters. He shares with Laín Entralgo and other core members of the generation of 1936 a thorough knowledge of Greek thought and scholastic philosophy as well as a familiarity with such moderns as Ortega, Heidegger and Zubiri. But unlike his colleagues, Aranguren is also drawn to British empiricism and the school of ordinary language analysis. Furthermore, he believes that in our time the positive sciences can furnish the essential knowledge necessary for the solution of basic social problems. Consequently, it is an impatience with metaphysics and a desire to fuse effectively theory and praxis that reveal Aranguren's affinity to socialist thinkers. "What matters most today," he avers, "is not an exchange of abstract notions, but that we give practical attention to the basic problems of our time."[1]

Aranguren has shown to be more responsive to the demands of secularization than his friend Laín, and his criticism of Spanish society, especially official Catholicism, has been bolder and more explicit than that of any Catholic member of his generation. This may be one of the reasons for his reservations about being considered an authentic member of the group of 1936. As Aranguren himself has observed: "I have arrived late, and this separates me somewhat, without my actually willing it, from my contemporaries (*coetáneos*) and places me closer to those who came later."[2] Indeed, Aranguren's unflagging encouragement, support and participation in university reform has earned him the respect and admiration of the new generation, to whom he has also addressed some of his most controversial essays.

Aranguren's main contribution to Spanish thought is a treatise on ethics titled *Etica,* which is so far the only book in Spain on moral science written in a rigorous, non-apologetic language of contemporary philosophy. In his introductory chapter the author of *Etica* affirms that man is constitutively moral by virtue of his need to interact with others and adjust *(ajustarse)* to situations. In this primary sense morality is a *structure* of coexistence and is conceived as an anthropological datum which is the ground of morality as *content*, that is, moral, immoral or amoral modes of behavior, depending on the value system of the individual. Man is moral in the anthropological sense of the word because his actions accrue an *ethos* or character; whether this character is ultimately judged as moral or immoral is another question. To accept morality as a structure is to recognize that all human activity is moral, and that likewise all disciplines which study basically or in an ancillary way forms of coexistence, such as political science, sociology, literature, etc., contain explicit or implicit ethical problems.[3]

It is not the purpose of this chapter to attempt a detailed analysis of Aranguren's contributions to ethics, but rather to point in a general way to his role as a moralist and to illustrate a transition in contemporary Spanish letters from academic to practical ethics. For in the essays of Aranguren we find a change in critical tone; a shift from the reserved, discriminating and elegant concern of a Laín, to the more direct accusatory posture of a moral witness, which falls short of an affiliation with any political cause.

Aranguren assigns to the intellectual in our time, and especially in Spain, the role of moralist, whose obligation is to become a spokesman for the most progressive and responsible segment of society. The intellectual-moralist should express as clearly, objectively and forcefully as possible, the moral exigencies of the historical period in which he lives through a relentless criticism of institutions and ideologies. While the moralist must work for a better society he must also maintain total intellectual independence. Or, as Aranguren puts it, it is his mission to forge the moral conscience of society by remaining both solitary and solidary: *"solidariamente solitario y solitariamente solidario."*[4] A moralist's role should not be political; rather, he should attempt to infuse political action with values and indicate the limits and possibilities of social programs. From Aranguren's perspective the social context of morality can never be programmed politically but is dictated by very specific human needs in which case morality acquires a practical function in response to what Ortega called *estar al nivel de los tiempos.*

*Practical Ethics*

A good illustration of practical ethics is Aranguren's participation in a student demonstration for university reform, which in 1965 cost him his job. Since the early 1950s the student body at the Central University, with the support of a handful of faculty members, has tried in vain to secure permission from the government to form their own organization. Since the end of the Civil War the authorities have made it obligatory for students to enroll in the government's own association (SEU), considered by most to be extremely restrictive and certainly outdated in its structure. On February 23, 1965, a group of students, accompanied by Aranguren decided to march peacefully to the dean and present a petition listing student demands for an autonomous association. When they were approaching the Rector's office, a law officer halted the marchers and demanded politely an explanation of the students' intentions. Informed of their desire to present a petition to the dean, the officer replied that he would soon return with instructions. This he soon did, though not to deliver a verbal message but to disperse the marchers, Aranguren included, with a powerful stream of water. Subsequently, Aranguren was dismissed from his chair of Ethics as were other professors at Madrid and elsewhere.

Aranguren did not accompany those students as a member of a political party nor did he do it in the name of revolution; he had given witness to the need of freedom of association.

*Awakening the Spanish Catholics*

Equally dramatic were Aranguren's efforts to revitalize Catholic thought in post-Civil War Spain. In 1953 he earned the vituperation of the neotraditionalist intellectuals and clerics for his *Catolicismo y Protestantismo como formas de existencia*[6] in which he pursued an unprejudiced study of the Protestant disposition or *talante* as he usually calls it. At the time of its publication any work dealing with heretics or unbelievers that fell short of total condemnation was considered anti-Spanish and contrary to the spirit of the "Crusade." In *Catolicismo día tras día*[7] (1955) Aranguren credits such heretics as Unamuno and Kierkegaard with having revived religious sentiment in our time and accuses Spanish Catholicism of complacency and intellectual sterility. In an number of essays in this volume he predicts the ever increasing role of the layman in the structure of religious life and enumerates the new demands made on believers in an age of secularization. Later, in *La juventud europea y otros ensayos*[8] (1961), he takes the Spanish Church to task for living in fear instead of hope and for attempting to absorb the political sphere of life into a concept of a spiritually homogeneous society.

In the early 1950s Aranguren was already courageously supporting the spirit of *aggiornamento* subsequently announced by John XXIII in 1962. And while some of his liberal contemporaries only began to recognize the social mission of Catholicism, Aranguren, as early as 1963, was already in full dialogue with Marxism. Our author predicts that the revolutionary fervor of the clergy will not be expressed politically but that it will reflect a genuine Christian consciousness: renunciation of power and the willingness to share their lives with the workers, guided by the spirit of Christ as "the man for others."[9]

## Humanism and Humanitarianism

Like Tierno Galván, Aranguren imputes to traditional humanism a lack of moral commitment to eliminate human suffering. If anything, humanism has been socially conservative and even reactionary. The sociological basis of classical humanism, for instance, was slavery, the most flagrant denial of human dignity. In the twentieth century, observes Aranguren, this form of inhumanity has taken the more sophisticated form of colonial exploitation.[10] It is interesting to note that the same year as Aranguren wrote this essay on humanism (1961), Sartre, in his preface to Franz Fanon's *The Wretched of the Earth*, explained that the violence and general instability of third world societies is a violence learned from European settlers who in the name of humanism lied, brutalized and pillaged. But, concludes Aranguren, whether one speaks of an institutionalized form of violence exercised by the status quo of repressive regimes, or a more direct revolutionary violence, it is in both cases still inhuman. A true humanism, therefore, will also have to be a humanitarianism which will oppose all violence.[11]

But recently, in response to the phenomena of increasing student protest and violent confrontations with the police, Aranguren has suggested that the problem of violence is more complex than he had once thought. Whether revolution has to be violent or non-violent is no longer a meaningful question because once the revolutionary process breaks loose collective behavior becomes manifest as a continuum in which violence and non-violence become indistinguishable.

Where, for example, does one draw the distinction between violence and non-violence in such provocative acts as the teasing, taunting and ridiculing of police by demonstrators? The strategy of contemporary revolutionaries is what the author calls, borrowing a term from a French sociologist, *contestation* which makes revolution a creative, on-going event, in which the elite and the masses, planning and action coincide. In contrast to the French Revolution, intellectuals and activists are no longer separable. Those who will act no longer wait for optimal objective conditions because those conditions are being continually created. *Contestation,* in short, means that today the revolutionary does not separate his beliefs from his actions; it is not, Aranguren insists, a unilaterally political, social or economic response, but a total response carried out by the whole man. Hence, it is impossible to formulate an ethic or a theology of revolution. This does not mean that one should not denounce injustice; it simply means that there are no general norms as to how far one is to carry this response or *contestation,* because "the ambiguity of all temporal action is insuperable and it is up to every individual to decide the degree of commitment to it."[12]

Is Aranguren apolitical? In a sense yes, if we think of politics as a mechanism for the acquisition of power. But if we think of politics in the broader sense, as a commitment to an ethic of coexistence, then Aranguren is indeed political.

## *Communication and the Illusion of Happiness*

Another task of the moralist in contemporary society is to help restore authenticity and honesty in human communication which has been trivialized and placed in the service of a consumer economy by the mass media. Traditionally, the ultimate function of ethics is personal happiness, which can only be achieved through self-knowledge manifest in the pursuit of a vocation. But today, claims Aranguren, society has fallen under the spell of a hedonistic ethic which is oriented not toward a personal perfection but instant gratification. Hedonism is a product of mass media; it provides a society of leisure with the illusion of happiness. In essence, what society consumes is publicity and advertisement disguised as information, a process in which the main channels of communication become the agents of mass culture, or "cultural-fiction" as Aranguren calls it. In a society of leisure the mass media creates needs and invents an imaginary, mythical world of glamorous personalities. Information becomes the mere by-product of a massive effort to nurture erotic fantasies and illusions of power. Obviously, happiness based on the escape from the real world is not really happiness, and the degradation of communication through mass media leads the moralist to oppose the values of a society of leisure and attempt to restore direct, authentic communication.[13]

## A Lexicon of Realities

There is scarcely a page in Aranguren's work that does not contain an italicized foreign word. Now, at least one reason why a writer would wish to employ a foreign word is because the phenomenon that he is describing, or the idea he wants to communicate, is not indigenous to his own culture. The fact that the foreign words to be found in Aranguren's essays are English is significant. Most of them represent sociological categories or are terms for cultural phenomena in highly industrialized societies. Although some of these words would be considered necessary to convey precise philosophical meaning, others, I believe, are unnecessary for the practical purposes of exposition and conceptual coherence. Yet these too serve a specific function, a rhetorical function if you will, as I will shortly indicate.

I open at random a book of Aranguren's essays and come across such words as *hobby, organization man, in-group and out-group, cross-cultures, adjustment, self-government, catchwords, mass-media, generalist, specialist.* All these are necessary if the conceptual context in which they are found is to be clear, and they must be drafted into Spanish sociological prose on the principle of efficacy in the transmission of ideas pertaining to a discipline organically bound to another culture. But then what of words, far more numerous than the above kind, such as *make sense, self-defeating prophecy, ways of life, monkish virtues, belief, honesty, booby-traps, victorian cant, means, training, privacy;* none of which are essential, or even minimally constructive, because their Spanish counterparts can capture the meaning with equal accuracy.

Aranguren's use of English sociological terms is a tribute to the Anglo-Saxon empirical tradition of intellectual rigor and modest aims, virtues he has long admired and practiced. As for his indulgence in non-technical words, it should be seen as an attempt to transplant into Spain the awareness of a foreign social consciousness. The author's technique is certainly not a plea for emulation of alien models of coexistence; it is an attempt to apprehend the life styles in highly industrialized societies. These anglicisms conjure up the spirit of the times, whatever its moral value, and transmit what Ortega called *el nivel de los tiempos.* Aranguren's predilection for an English vocabulary is not a faddish exercise nor a sign of petulance; these words are not literal expressions but symbolic gestures; they are an index or *representations* of a cultural reality designed to create awareness. Ultimately it is a reflection of Aranguren's total immersion in the social realities of our time.

## *One Step to the Left: Castilla del Pino as Moralist*

Carlos Castilla del Pino, director since 1949 of the neuro-psychiatric center of Córdoba, is a Marxist who dedicated one of his major works to Aranguren. The inscription reads: "to a professor of Ethics, for whom the subject is not only academic but also practical." It seems fitting, I think, to conclude this chapter with a brief note on Castilla's role as a moralist.

Castilla del Pino's writings fall into two categories, works of popularization and studies in psychiatry and philosophical anthropology. His works of vulgarization are essentially paraphrases of Marx's early essays, especially the *Economic and Philosophical Manuscripts of 1844,* and serve the very specific and conscious purpose of acquainting the Spanish public with Socialist thought in the hope that it will generate a revolutionary consciousness.[14] Of the author's academic endeavors should be mentioned, first and foremost, *Un estudio sobre la depresión: fundamentos de antropología dialéctica* (1966) and *La culpa* (1968). The study of depression is the first work of its kind in Spain to make use of Marxist categories with the explicit aim of transcending what Castilla believes are the limitations of a personalist concept of medicine. A therapeutic method based on a dialectical anthropology starts with the premise that neurotic behavior can be adequately explained only when considered within the social structure, or *situación* in which it occurs.[15] Rof Carballo has already described the transactional relationship in which he emphasized the individual's mutual modification in parental relationships. Castilla enlarges this concept with the analytic tools of Marxism and stresses the sociogenic nature of character formation.

Likewise, Castilla offers a corrective to the existential and psychoanalytic views of such phenomena as alienation and guilt. For example, guilt does not have for the author an ontological status; it is not merely a consequence of existence. Guilt is not just of someone, but essentially before others: "Through guilt man becomes conscious not only of the fact that he is with others—those who reveal to him his guilt—but also of the fact that he has to live with others and do what is expected of him."[16] The origin of guilt is therefore social, even if the experience itself is personal.

In his critique of traditional humanism Castilla radicalizes Aranguren's concept of practical ethics in the sense that he defines the role of the moralist more clearly in political terms, that is, within the context of a Marxist ideology. But more interesting and relevant is the author's view of personal ethics. Like Ortega, Laín and Aranguren, Castilla too addresses himself to the question of vocation. Ortega's frequent reference to life as *intimidad,* as drama, and as the projection of our imaginary self, indicates a personalist, existential terminology which captures only the internal dialectic between the self and the ideal self; a dialectic confined to a biographical, subjective structure of existence and sustained by such traditional humanist virtues as courage and magnanimity. But Castilla, a Marxist, considers this notion of vocation to be a mere abstraction; he holds that the viability of a personal project and the chance of its fulfillment depend as much on circumstances as on personal resolve. Furthermore, the efficacy and validity of a personal project are tested ultimately in praxis, that is in work: "Man's project is his praxis, within his reality, through which he unfolds whatever he considers possible for himself in a given situation."[17]

At this point one is tempted to interject a defense of Ortega and cite, as one of many examples, his study of Velázquez where chance *(azar)* and circumstances, as well as the notion of an ideal self form the substance of a personal vocation.[18] Ortega, I think, understood quite well the concept of self-alienation, a concept so frequently invoked by Marxists, but he did express it too often in purely personalist terms. But there are times when he comes close to Castilla's view and recognizes that the "I" is only a small part of that radical reality that is one's life. In *Prólogo para alemanes* he states that "whatever truly is is my coexistence with things."[19] It is not accurate therefore, for Castilla to say that in the works of Ortega there is a constant disdain of circumstances in favor of the ideal self.[20]

If for Aranguren the intellectual must pass from humanism to a humanitarianism, yet remain politically neutral, Castilla exhorts the reader to action. In *La culpa,* in a random sample of two pages one finds exhortations such as these: "One must do otherwise right here and now. . . .What one must overcome in the process is indecision which springs from a fear of falling back on an erroneous path. . . . One must do what one ought to do within the limits of the possible. . . One must make everyone conscious of the need for action."[21] As in Tierno Galván so in the prose of Castilla we find a rich lexicon of the social sciences. The factual reality described by science is bound to certain desirable goals and thus Castilla's exhortations to action is a call to fulfill the logic of history generated by dialectical materialism. Rhetoric in this sense attempts to bridge the gap between what can be known and the possibilities for happiness.

# CONCLUSION

Tierno's remark that the world is not the dwelling place of man is the strongest conceivable indictment of conservative humanism. For indeed, Tierno is determined to close that "psychological distance from which we oppose the world" and lead us to submit totally to the reality of the external world. He holds that as long as we remain oriented toward an interior self and seek knowledge in self-analysis, abstract thought, dialogue and intuition, we are confined to a world of fictions.

Yet it is precisely this interior world of man as subject—the state of solitude—which traditional humanists consider the most exalted state of self-consciousness and the source of true knowledge. For Laín and Rof solitude is that inner state which enables the morally aware individual to mobilize his spiritual resources and experience an affinity with mankind. Hence, Laín's paradoxical comment "*cuanto más solo más acompañado,*" and Rof's remark that a capacity for solitude is "*el logro supremo del hombre.*" On the other hand, for Marxists like Castilla and Tierno the need for solitude is not the most radically human propensity because man is essentially a communal being. Consequently, reality is not an inner state but human action verified in the world, an action not dependent on ethical problem-solving but on the analysis and control of external contingencies.

Where Castilla can still affirm "man in his reality" and propound a "realistic humanism," Tierno considers all anthropological categories obsolete and replaces the concept of person with that of social structure. In this sense he differs radically from the rest of the essayists considered in this study who assume that man has a nature manifest in the individual's sense of uniqueness, freedom and moral responsibility which constitute his dignity as a person. Even Castilla's concrete anthropology, dependent as it is on scientific methods of verification, retains the notion of the subject as a moral agent. But as Tierno sees it, even a realistic humanism such as Castilla's, which stresses man's practical role in social transformation and seeks to close the gap between human and inhuman, and authentic and inauthentic forms of existence can outlive its usefulness. The theoretical support of a philosophical anthropology is no longer needed because it is no longer *man's project* that is of consequence but the *destiny of the species embodied in society.* Thus, the revolutionary process itself has absorbed and dissolved the concept of human nature.

This novel concept of the relation between individual and society also leads Tierno to revise the function of imagination. The very core of philosophical anthropology, as we have seen, is the category of project, in which the imagination plays a decisive role. Ortega spoke to the point when he noted that man is an impossibility without imagination, without a capacity to invent for himself the substance and style of his life. For the philosopher of vital reason "man is the novelist of himself."

Tierno on the other hand would say that there is no longer a private, unique life to invent, because there is not—should not be—an autonomous "I" to choose a way of being. The existential-historicist categories of biography and vocation so dear to Ortega have lost their function for Tierno. Man does not invent his destiny; rather he adjusts to facts, and engineers and controls his destiny in accordance with the possibilities of dialectical reason. Therefore, if the inventive faculties are not subordinated to utility and the creation of deployable social models, their products remain without epistemological status and relegated to the category of the esthetic dimension. Tierno would not accept Ortega's contention that scientific formulas and models are not very different from metaphors; because the former are deployable whereas a pure metaphor remains a fiction with no practical consequences.

Following up the theme of invention and imagination, it would be interesting to compare Tierno and Rof Carballo on the subject of demythification. In accordance with his Marxist view of society, Tierno means by demythification *(desmitologización)* the unmasking of the false consciousness of those who seek to perpetuate their interests by defending an anachronistic ideology. Mythification is a form of subjective falsification of reality which becomes more pervasive in proportion to the weakening of an ideology. Now these falsifications are, in Marxist terminology, not ideas corresponding to reality but derivative ideas, reflecting the interests of either the ruling class or the ambivalences of confused or cowardly intellects.

For Rof myth is a mode of man's quest for identity, a representation of individual and collective experience which can both communicate self-knowledge and link the individual to the numinous. But modern man in his arrogance and perverse rational pride has become blind to transcendence and through a process of self-deification has deformed the spiritual import of universal myths. Rof's operative concept of demythification serves to recover the pristine, life-enhancing meaning and power of Christian symbolism by stripping it of cultural deformations and scientific reductionism. Rof too wants to expose a false consciousness and show that man is not really what he thinks he is. Man is deluded by the illusory power of operational reason: knowledge which enables him to calculate, manipulate and control the external world has also made him dangerously self-centered, arrogantly autonomous, personally rootless and spiritually truncated. Where Rof wants to recover an image of man, Tierno's vision is totally futuristic. Rof traces the causes of inhumanity to personal frailty and ignorance, Tierno to the economic basis of coexistence.

Leaving political inclinations apart, Tierno's philosophical orientation is very similar to the theories of B.F. Skinner. Speaking on the relation between behaviorism and humanism, the world's leading behaviorist, who also prefers "the species" to man, has made the following observations:

> It is often said that a behavioristic analysis "dehumanizes man." But it merely dispenses with harmful explanatory fiction. In doing so it moves much more directly toward the goals that fiction was designed, erroneously, to serve.

> If we are to solve the problems that face us in the world today, this concern for mental life must no longer divert our attention from the environmental contingencies of which human behavior is a function.

Can this kind of philosophy take root in Spain? Will cold, objective analysis and the total control of human behavior ever prove compatible with the so-called Spanish character, with its propensity for passionate belief rather than rationalism, with its pride in "men of flesh and bone?" Or is Tierno the new "iron surgeon" who wants to extirpate from the body of Spanish culture such shibboleths as the esthetic notions of national character and destiny, an indulgent disdain for science and an undying devotion to individualism. Surely if Unamuno's personalism and Ortega's vital reason are uniquely Spanish then the work of Tierno is an alien philosophy in the history of Peninsular thought. Do Ortega and Tierno have anything in common? The philosopher of vital reason wished to transcend metaphysics, and attempted to formulate a science of reality; but there is a wide gap between a man who asserts that "the radical reality is my life" and a man for whom the possessive "my" is of little worth. Nevertheless, a meeting of minds between Ortega's disciples and Marxists could be mutually beneficial; a philosophy of vital reason could check Tierno's foolhardy acceptance of scientific absolutism, and a theory of praxis could awaken the social responsibility of the Spanish intellectual, immersed in the humanistic tradition.

The reader may have detected a degree of enthusiasm for Tierno which is not shown for other essayists. This is not a sign of agreement with the author's analysis of society nor an endorsement of his ideology. However, I do believe that of the writers treated in this study Tierno fulfills the role of the essayist best. His thought is marked by an intellectual verve and boldness which make for consistently interesting reading. He seems to be the first essayist of stature in post-Civil War Spain who enjoys working with ideas unencumbered by psychological limitations. Tierno's chief virtue consists in an inexhaustible capacity for brilliant insight and surprise, traits reminiscent of Ortega. Some of his contemporaries, on both sides of the Atlantic, may prove superior in erudition, elegance, and even wisdom. But the vigor, lucidity, and depth of Tierno's thought place him in the select company of Américo Castro, Francisco Ayala, and Juan David García-Bacca.

# NOTES

## Introduction

[1]Pedro Laín Entralgo, "Por la integridad de España," in *Ejercicios de comprensión* (Madrid, 1959), p. 55.

[2]José Ortega y Gasset, *Obras completas* VIII (Madrid, 1965), p. 52.

[3]Juan Marichal, *La voluntad de estilo* (Barcelona, 1957), p. 14.

[4]Theodor W. Adorno, "El ensayo como forma," *Notas de literatura* (Barcelona, 1962), pp. 19-20.

[5]Jaime Giordano, "Feijoo y el género ensayístico," *Grial* (Vigo), nov.-dic., 1970, p. 410.

[6]Ciriaco Morón Arroyo, *El sistema de Ortega y Gasset* (Madrid, 1968), p. 52.

[7]*Obras completas* I, p. 318.

[8]Kenneth Burke, *A Rhetoric of Motives* (New York, 1955), p. 27.

[9]Robert G. Mead, Jr., *Breve historia del ensayo hispanoamericano* (México, 1956), pp. 8-9.

[10]Discussed in James Willis Robb's *El estilo de Alfonso Reyes* (México, 1965), p. 16.

[11]See chapter IV.

[12]Pedro Laín Entralgo, *España como problema* (Madrid, 1962), p. xix.

[13]José Luis Aranguren, *Memorias y esperanzas españolas* (Madrid, 1969), p. 220.

[14]Richard M. Weaver, "The *Phaedrus* and the Nature of Rhetoric," in *Philosophy, Rhetoric and Argumentation*, Maurice Natanson and Henry Johnstone, eds. (Pennsylvania State University Press), p. 75.

[15]Pedro Laín Entralgo, *La curación por la palabra en la antigüedad clásica* (Madrid, 1958), p. 249.

[16]"La generación del 36," *Symposium*, Summer, 1968.

[17]Julián Marías, Forward to Guillermo Díaz-Plaja's *Memorias de una generación destruida (1930-1936)*, (Barcelona, 1966), p. 6.

[18]Vicente Marrero, *La guerra española y el trust de cerebros* (Madrid, 1962), p. 25.

[19]There are two doctoral dissertations on Laín: Pedro Soler Puigoriol, *El hombre, ser indigente: El pensamiento antropológico de Pedro Laín Entralgo* (Madrid: Guadarrama, 1966), and my own unpublished Ph.D. thesis, *El humanismo de Pedro Laín Entralgo* (University of Connecticut, 1968). I have learned that Professor Donald Bleznick of the University of Cincinnati is now preparing a book-length study of Laín's work.

[20]Helio Carpintero, *Cinco aventuras españolas* (Laín, Aranguren, Marías, Ferrater Mora, F. Ayala), (Revista de Occidente, 1967). After our present study had been submitted for publication, Elías Díaz published a series of articles in *Sistema* (January, 1973; May, 1973; October, 1973) with the title "Notas para una historia del pensamiento español actual (1939-72)," which subsequently appeared in book form (Editorial Cuadernos para el diálogo, 1974).

subsequently appeared in book form (Editorial Cuadernos para el diálogo, 1974).

# Chapter I.

[1]Carlos Mainer, "*Vértice* en la vida literaria de su tiempo," *Insula*, 252 (1967), p. 3.

[2]Kessel Schwarts, "Culture and the Spanish Civil War—A Fascist View," *Journal of Inter-American Studies*, 4 (1965). Included in *The Meaning of Existence in Contemporary Hispanic Literature* (U. of Miami Press, 1969), pp. 197-218.

[3]Walter Benjamin, *Illuminations* (New York, 1969), p. 241.

[4]Ibid., pp. 241-42.

[5]"José Antonio Primo de Rivera habla del fascismo," *ABC*, 22 de marzo, 1933; recogido por Fernando Díaz-Plaja en *La historia de España en sus documentos: el siglo XX (1923-36)*, Instituto de Estudios Políticos (Madrid, 1964), p. 589.

[6]Here are a few samples from Giménez' *Los secretos de la Falange* (Barcelona, 1939). "En 1933 el 'Verbo' se hizo ya Doctrina." p. 12; "La Falange de Franco asumirá la misión universal que predicó Cristo en el mundo," p. 22; "Intelectuales—los que andan con la cabeza abajo: ¡heterodoxos, sofistas, herejes, pedantes, intelectuales!," p. 40; "Hitler: el iluminado de un destino romántico en el mundo," p. 89. For further examples of extravagant ultra-conservative rhetoric see José María Pemán's poem *La bestia y el ángel*, partially reproduced in Vicente Marrero's *La guerra española y el trust de cerebros* (Madrid, 1962); Enrique Suñer, *Los intelectuales y la tragedia española* (Burgos, 1937); Wenceslao González Oliveros, *Falange y Requeté, orgánicamente solidarios* (Valladolid, 1937).

[7]Giménez Caballero, *Arte y estado* (Madrid, 1935), p. 68. A repentant Vanguardist, Giménez deprecates Modernism: "la reprehensible tendencia moderna. . .la escultura del hombre-máquina, el culto de lo primitivo, lo infra-humano, lo ínfimo. . .proviene de ese instinto diabólico de imitar a Dios," p. 124.

[8]Angel María Pascual, "Quadrivio imperial," *Jerarquía*, 1 (1936). The magazine had various subtitles, such as "Guía del Imperio de la Sabiduría, de los Oficios" and "La revista negra de la Falange." Its epigraphic style contained vows such as "Para Dios y el César" and "A Roma por todo." Frequent contributors were Ors himself, his disciple Basterra, Fermín Izurdiaga Lorca and such early Heideggerians as Laín and García Valdecasas.

[9]*Escorial*, 1 (1940), p. 11.

[10]*Escorial*, 10 (1942), p. 40.

[11]Albert Speer, *Inside the Third Reich: Memoirs* (New York, 1970). Chapter on "Architectural Megalomania."

[12]Pedro Laín Entralgo, "El teatro de Gonzalo Torrente," *Vestigios: En-*

*sayos de crítica y amistad* (Madrid, 1948), p. 101.

[13]Giménez, *Los secretos*. . .The author speaks of a reprehensible "señoritismo y la frívola traición del hijo àl padre: el avergonzarse de los esfuerzos paternales," p. 87.

[14]*El viaje del joven Tobías* (Pamplona, 1938). Asmodeo is given lines such as "¡Bah! ¡contra todos los ángeles mi truco del complejo de Electra no falla! ¡Es una maravilla! p. 51; "Lo sé todo, estudié psicoanálisis," p. 41. Torrente follows closely the Orsian notion of dialogue and dialectic. "Diálogo hay"—writes Ors—"cuando en un libro. . .aquel que establece una tesis y la sustenta prevé las objeciones posibles y anticipadamente mide su alcance, quita su fuerza, extirpa su malicia, destruye or reduce su eficacia." *Una lección de filosofía*. Cited by Aranguren in *La filosofía de Eugenio d'Ors* (Madrid, 1945), p. 112-13.

[15]Antonio Tovar, "Antígona y el tirano, o la inteligencia en la política," *Escorial*, 10 (1942), p. 50.

[16]Ibid., p. 51.

[17]Eugenio d'Ors, *Poussin y el Greco* (Madrid, 1922), pp. 15, 128.

[18]Eugenio Montes, "El sueño de la razón," *Escorial*, 1 (1940), pp. 16-18. The idea that traditional values are being devoured by Technology and Progress was also a favorite topic of Falangists like Agustín de Foxá, Juan Aparicio and Rafael Sánchez Mazas, who were regular contributors to *Vértice*.

[19]G. Torrente Ballester, *El casamiento engañoso* (Madrid, 1941).

[20]G. Torrente Ballester, *República Barataria* (Madrid, 1942).

[21]*La filosofía de Eugenio d'Ors*, p. 265.

[22]In *Jerarquía*, 4 (1937), Laín has an article on "Quevedo y Heidegger." In another essay, "Meditación apasionada sobre el estilo de la Falange" (*Jerarquía*, 2 (1937), p. 168), Laín writes: "El ser-para-la-muerte lo hemos escrito y vivido los españoles más que nadie. Con más intensidad, pero con distinto sentido: porque nuestra serie analítica no termina en Temporalidad—ser-para-la-muerte-Ex nihilo, sino en Temporalidad—Ser-para-la-muerte-A Deo. . . .A la metafísica de la angustia opone el español. . .esa metafísica de la alegría de que me ha hablado más de una vez Luis Rosales, el poeta."

[23]J.J. López Ibor, "El pathos ético del hombre español," *Escorial*, 3 (1941), p. 76.

[24]*Escorial*, 18 (1945), p. 175.

[25]Laín, quotes Dawson's *Los orígenes de Europa*: "Sentimos otra vez la necesidad de una unidad espiritual. . . .Advertimos la insuficiencia de una cultura puramente occidental y humanística." *Vestigios*, p. 482. Article written in 1945.

[26]Raúl Morodo, "Notas sobre la vida intelectual," *Esa gente de España: Estudios y documentos* (México, 1965), p. 27.

[27]See John R. Harrison, *The Reactionaries: A Study of the Anti-Democratic Intelligentsia* (New York, 1967).

[28]See Gonzalo Sobejano, *Nietzsche en España* (Madrid, 1966). In addition, Laín's "Sermón de la tarea nueva: mensaje a los intelectuales católicos" (*Jerarquía*, 1): "En el orden intelectual es preciso, es urgente acentuar la nota de la rebeldía. . . .Es preciso purificar nuestras mentes y nuestros corazones, y para ello nada mejor que una cristiana rebeldía contra todos los posos de cobarde adocenamiento que depositó sobre aquellos un siglo de vida

escindida y falsa," p. 44. "Uno ha de vivir incómodo, ha de huir de sentirse satisfecho. . . .Nuestra misión de intelectuales católicos es vivir en peligro, movernos en aquella zona de la verdad natural lindante con el error," p. 50.

# Chapter II.

[1] *Palabras menores* (Barcelona, 1952), p. 126.

[2] *La espera y la esperanza: historia y teoría del esperar humano* (Madrid, 1962), p. 551.

[3] *Obras* (Madrid, 1965), pp. 1137-51. The essay under discussion is "Picasso, problema y misterio."

[4] *La espera y la esperanza*, p. 568.

[5] Ibid., pp. 514-19.

[6] *La empresa de ser hombre* (Madrid, 1963), pp. 159-75.

[7] Ibid., p. 267.

[8] Ibid., p. 267-8.

[9] *España como problema* (Madrid, 1962), p. 670.

[10] Ibid.

[11] Ibid., p. 673.

[12] Ibid., p. 670.

[13] *Ejercicios de comprensión* (Madrid, 1959), pp. 15-16.

[14] *The Critique of Humanism: A Symposium*, C.H. Grattan, ed. (New York, 1968), p. 160.

[15] "Aranguren, humanista," *Cuadernos para el diálogo*, abril, 1966, pp. 27-28.

[16] "Hipocratismo, Neohipocratismo, Transhipocratismo," *Archivo iberoamericano de historia de la medicina*, XVI, 1964, p. 7.

[17] Humanism defined as a "quest for value" is found in Albert Levi's *Humanism and Politics* (Indiana University Press, 1969).

[18] *Enfermedad y pecado* (Barcelona, 1959), p. 49.

[19] See Richard M. Zaner, "An Approach to Philosophical Anthropology," *Philosophy and Phenomenological Research*, XXVII, 1966, p. 60.

[20] *La espera y la esperanza*, p. 551.

[21] *Obras*, p. 1130.

[22] Ibid., p. 1132.

[23] "Notas para una teoría de la lectura," in *Mis mejores páginas* (Madrid, 1968), p. 330.

[24] Ibid.

[25] "Sermón de la tarea nueva: mensaje a los intelectuales católicos," *Jerarquía* (Pamplona) I, 1936, p. 50.

[26] "La servidumbre de la cultura española," in *Sobre la cultura española* (Madrid, 1943), p. 141.

[27] See Stanley Payne, *Falange: A History of Spanish Fascism* (Stanford University Press), p. 243.

28Enrique Tierno Galván, "Los intelectuales en la España contemporánea," *Puerto*, oct-dic., 1967, pp. 24-28.

29Ibid.

30*Vestigios: ensayos de crítica y amistad* (Madrid, 1948), p. 437.

31*España como problema*, p. 676.

32*Obras*, p. 1200.

33*Entre nosotros* (Madrid, 1967).

34I am indebted here to A. Levi's discussion of Camus' humanism. See note 17 above.

35*Cuando se espera* (Madrid, 1967), p. 44.

36Albert Camus, *Les Justes* (Paris, Gallimard, 1950), pp. 76-77.

37*Cuando se espera*, pp. 65-66.

38*Obras*, p. 1107.

39Ibid., 1119.

40Chaim Perelman and L. Olbrechts-Tyteca, *The New Rhetoric* (University of Notre Dame Press, 1969), p. 79.

41George Santayana, *The Birth of Reason and Other Essays* (New York, 1968), p. 80.

42*Entre nosotros*, p. 117.

43Jorge Mañach, *Visitas españolas* (Madrid, 1960), p. 106.

44*Ejercicios de comprensión*, p. 51.

45Ibid., p. 50.

46*Mysterium doloris: hacia una teología cristiana de la enfermedad* (Madrid, 1955), pp. 9-11.

47*La espera y la esperanza*, p. 370.

48Pierre Teilhard de Chardin, *The Phenomenon of Man* (New York, 1965), p. 231.

49Ibid., p. 258.

50Ibid., p. 287.

51James Collins, *The Emergence of Philosophy of Religion* (Yale, 1967), p. 479.

# Chapter III.

1José Ortega y Gasset, "Psicoanálisis, ciencia problemática," *Obras completas*, I (Madrid, 1963), pp. 216-37.

2Sigmund Freud, "History of the Psychoanalytic Movement," in *The Basic Writings of Sigmund Freud* (New York, 1938), pp. 950-52.

3Juan Rof Carballo, "La nebulosa de la novela," *Papeles de Son Armadans*, XLIX (Junio, 1968), pp. 229-262. Also, Alvaro Fernández Suárez, *España, árbol vivo* (Madrid, 1962).

4Gregorio Marañón, *Raíz y decoro de España* (Madrid, 1933), p. 193. In a much earlier work ("Los estados intersexuales en la especie humana," 1919) he did recognize the importance of Freud, but on the whole he was, to say the least, ambivalent. As Gary D. Keller points out in his forthcoming book on *The Significance and Impact of Gregorio Marañón* (New York, Bilingual Press): "In addition to the harm that might befall his professional credentials the doctor was genuinely repulsed by some of the philosophic outcomes of Freudian psychology."

[5]Pío Baroja, *El escritor según él y según los críticos* (Madrid, 1944), p. 140.

[6]*Juan de Mairena*, II (Buenos Aires, 1968), p. 38.

[7]*Mis poemas mejores* (Madrid, 1961), p. 31.

[8]*The Secret Life of Salvador Dalí* (New York, 1942).

[9]"Freud y los surrealistas," *El sol*, 31 de julio, 1936.

[10]Francisco Marco Merenciano, *Fronteras de la locura: tres personajes de Azorín vistos por un psiquiatra* (Valencia, 1947).

[11]Juan J. López Ibor, *Lo vivo y lo muerto del psicoanálisis* (Madrid, 1936); *La agonía del psicoanálisis* (Madrid, 1951).

[12]*Estudios de la historia de la medicina y de la antropología médica* (Madrid, 1943).

[13]Ibid., p. 184.

[14]Ibid., p. 270.

[15]Ibid., p. 278.

[16]José Ferrater Mora, "Nota sobre Sigmund Freud," *La escuela activa* No. I, Habana, sept., 1939. Cited by María Zambrano (see below).

[17]"El freudismo, testimonio del hombre actual," *Hacia un saber sobre el alma* (Buenos Aires, 1950).

[18]For detailed discussion of the notion of *urdimbre* see *Violencia y ternura* (Madrid, 1967), pp. 23-42; "La situación contemporánea de la comprensión médica del hombre," *Boletín de patología médica*, VII, dic., 1967, pp. 234-54.

[19]*Violencia y ternura*, pp. 47-52.

[20]Paul Ricoeur, *Freud and Philosophy: An Essay on Interpretation* (Yale, 1970).

[21]Ibid., p. 410 ff; *Violencia y ternura*, 220.

[22]*Urdimbre afectiva y enfermedad* (Barcelona y Madrid, 1961), pp. 234-54.

[23]Ibid., p. 244.

[24]*Violencia y ternura*, p. 279.

[25]Ibid., p. 157.

[26]Ibid., p. 216.

[27]Ibid., p. 156.

[28]Ibid., pp. 281-90.

[29]Ibid., p. 290.

[30]Ibid., p. 281.

[31]Xavier Zubiri, *Naturaleza, Historia y Dios* (Madrid, 1963), pp. 368-403.

[32]*Violencia y ternura*, p. 275.

[33]Ibid.

[34]*Cerebro interno y mundo emocional* (Barcelona, 1952), p. 339.

[35]*Violencia y ternura*, p. 277.

[36]*Rebelión y futuro* (Madrid, 1970), p. 250.

[37]Ibid., p. 252.

[38]*Violencia y ternura*, p. 227.

[39]Ricoeur, op. cit., p. 543.

[40]"La nebulosa de la novela," loc. cit., p. 260.

[41]*Urdimbre afectiva*, pp. 481-85.

[42]Ibid., p. 486.

[43]*Violencia y ternura*, p. 277.

[44]Joseph Campbell, *The Masks of God: Creative Mythology* (New York, 1970), p. 4.

[45]*Cerebro interno*, p. 401.

[46]*Rebelión y futuro*, pp. 217-18.

[47]*Violencia y ternura*, p. 212.

[48]Kenneth Burke, *A Rhetoric of Motives* (New York, 1955), p. 87.

[49]Justina Ruíz de Conde, "La revolución matrista de Segismundo," *La torre*, año XI (oct-dic., 1963), pp. 93-106.

# Chapter IV.

## Abbreviations

| | |
|---|---|
| DET | *Desde el espectáculo a la trivialización*: Madrid, Taurus, 1961. |
| RR | *La realidad como resultado*: Boletín informativo del seminario de derecho político de la Universidad de Salamanca, 1959. |
| TM | *Tradición y modernismo*: Madrid, Tecnos, 1962. |
| DCP | *Diderot como pretexto*: Madrid, Taurus, 1965. |
| CCS | *Conocimiento y ciencias sociales*: Madrid, Tecnos, 1966. |
| RM | *Razón mecánica y razón dialéctica*: Madrid, Tecnos, 1969. |
| HR | *La humanidad reducida*: Madrid, Taurus, 1970. |
| A | *Acotaciones a la historia de la cultura occidental en la edad moderna*: Madrid, Tecnos, 1964. |

[1]Tierno, "Humanismo y sociedad," *La Torre*, Año 11 (enero-marzo, 1963), pp. 87-109.

[2]Ibid., p. 108.

[3]"Diálogo con el profesor Enrique Tierno Galván," *Ruedo Ibérico* (París), junio-julio, 1965.

[4]Tierno has shown no interest in phenomenology. The omission may be an indication that he considers it of little use as a tool of social epistemology Likewise, the philosophy of vital reason, in itself a kind of phenomenology, has made no impression on Tierno, and he must consider the Orteguian tradition as another form of *literaturización*.

[5]Julián Marías, "Spain is in Europe," *Books Abroad*, Summer, 1952.

[6]Tierno, *Anatomía de la conspiración* (Madrid, Taurus, 1962), p. 50.

[7]Theodor W. Adorno, "El ensayo como forma," *Notas de literatura* (Barcelona, Ariel, 1962), p. 21.

**Thomas Mermall**

[8]Tierno, *El tacitismo en las doctrinas políticas del siglo de oro español* (Murcia, 1949).

[9]Juan Marichal, *El nuevo pensamiento político español* (México, 1966), pp. 37-38.

[10]Francis Bacon, *The Advancement of Learning*, Book I.

[11]Francis Bacon, *Novum Organum*, Aphorism LIX.

[12]A personal or ethical humanism among some socialists would imply from the Marxist point of view (and in this case from Tierno's) a contradiction. As Luis Althusser has pointed out, if man is a system of social relations, then such theoretical trappings as human nature or essence are superfluous and unscientific. See Althusser's article "Marxismo y humanismo," *Cristianos y marxistas: Los problemas de un diálogo* (Madrid, Alianza Editorial, 1969), p. 180.

[13]Manuel Tuñón de Lara, *Medio siglo de cultura española* (Madrid, Tecnos, 1971), pp. 93, 162-87, 214.

[14]Ganivet, *Idearium español* in *Obras completas* I (Madrid, Aguilar, 1961), pp. 211-212.

# Chapter V.

[1]*Implicaciones de la filosofía en la vida contemporánea* (Madrid: Taurus, 1963), p. 39.

[2]*Crítica y meditación* (Madrid: Taurus, 1957), p. 133.

[3]*Etica* (Madrid: Revista de Occidente, 1963), pp. 54-74.

[4]"El oficio del moralista en la sociedad actual," *Papeles de Son Armadans*, XL, 1959, p. 111.

[5]*Memorias y esperanzas españolas* (Madrid: Taurus, 1969), pp. 169-74.

[6]Madrid; Revista de Occidente, 1952.

[7]Barcelona: Noguer, 1955.

[8]Barcelona: Seix-Barral, 1961.

[9]*Memorias y esperanzas españolas*, p. 213.

[10]"Sobre el humanismo," *Obras* (Madrid: Plenitud, 1965), pp. 883-96.

[11]Ibid., p. 890.

[12]*Memorias y esperanzas españolas*, pp. 152-57.

[13]"Problemas éticos y morales en la comunicación humana," *Revista de Occidente*, enero, 1972, pp. 22-24. For a more detailed discussion see Aranguren's *Human Communication* (New York: McGraw-Hill, 1969).

[14]Examples are: *El humanismo 'imposible'* (Madrid: Editorial Ciencia Nueva, 1968); *La alienación de la mujer* (Madrid: Editorial Ciencia Nueva, 1968); *Naturaleza del saber* (Madrid: Taurus, 1970).

[15]*Un estudio sobre la depresión: fundamentos de antropología dialéctica* (Barcelona: Ediciones Península, primera edición, 1966), p. 53.

[16]*La culpa* (Madrid: Revista de Occidente, 1968), p. 56.

[17]Ibid., p. 34.

[18]José Ortega y Gasset, *Obras completas* VI, p. 422; VIII, p. 467.
[19]Ibid., VIII, p. 51.
[20]*La culpa*, p. 105.
[21]Ibid., pp. 274-75.

# Conclusion

[1]B.F. Skinner, "Humanism and Behaviorism," *The Humanist*, July-August, 1972, pp. 19-20.

# BIBLIOGRAPHY

Complete, or nearly complete bibliographies are available on the works of Aranguren, Laín Entralgo and Rof Carballo. The following sources may be consulted. For Aranguren: *Teoría y sociedad: homenaje al profesor Aranguren* (ensayos compilados por F. Gracia, J. Muguerza y V. Sánchez de Zavala). Barcelona: Ariel, 1970. For Laín Entralgo: Thomas Mermall, *El humanismo de Pedro Laín Entralgo.* Doctoral thesis, University of Connecticut, 1968. Helio Carpintero, *Cinco aventuras españolas.* Madrid: Revista de Occidente, 1967. For Rof Carballo: *Hacia una nueva endocrinología:* discurso para la recepción pública del académico electo Excmo. Sr. D. Juan Rof Carballo, leído el día 4 de marzo de 1969. Real Academia Nacional de Medicina.

To my knowledge no one has compiled a bibliography of the works of Tierno Galván and Castilla del Pino. Titles supplementary to the works cited at the end of chapters IV and V are included in the General Bibliography.

## English translations of original works

Aranguren, J.L. *Human communication.* New York: McGraw-Hill, 1969

Laín Entralgo, Pedro. "An Approach to a Theology of Illness," in *Mind and Body.* Kenedy, Harvill, 1955.

_____. *Doctor and Patient.* New York: McGraw-Hill, 1969.

_____. *The Therapy of the Word in Classical Antiquity.* New Haven: Yale, 1970.

Caponigri, Robert (ed.). *Contemporary Spanish Philosophy: An Anthology.* Notre Dame University Press, 1967.

*The Texas Quarterly.* Special issue dedicated to the "Image of Spain." Austin: The University of Texas, 1961. Contains essays by Aranguren, Laín, Marías and others.

## A selected critical bibliography of the contemporary Spanish essays and the history of ideas

Abellán, José Luis. *La cultura en España* (Ensayo para un diagnóstico). Madrid: Cuadernos para el diálogo, 1971. Contains the author's review articles in *Insula* from 1966-1971.

Ayala, Francisco. *Razón del mundo: la preocupación de España.* Xalapa, Universidad Veracruzana, 1962.

_____."España a la fecha." *Cuadernos Americanos* (sept.-oct.,1964), pp. 46-80.

Calvo-Serer, Rafael. *España sin problema.* Madrid: Rialp, 1957. The neo-traditionalist view of contemporary Spanish history. In recent years the author has moved to a conservative liberal position.

Carpintero, Helio. *Cinco aventuras españolas* (Ayala, Laín, Aranguren, Ferrater, Marías). Madrid: Revista de Occidente, 1967. Introductory essays, essentially expository.

*Cuadernos para el diálogo,* XIV, mayo, 1969. Número extraordinario: "Treinta años de literatura. Narrativa y poesía española, 1939-1969."

Díaz, Elías. "La filosofía marxista en el pensamiento español actual." *Cuadernos para el diálogo,* LXIII, diciembre, 1968.

_____.*Notas para una historia del pensamiento español actual (1939-1972).* Madrid: Cuadernos para el diálogo, 1974. Originally published in shorter form in the journal *Sistema,* numbers 1 (enero, 1973), 2 (mayo, 1973) and 3 (octubre, 1973). This is the most comprehensive and conscientious treatment of post Civil War intellectual history, marked by professor Díaz' usual perspicacity.

Fernández de la Mora, Gonzalo. The author is the regular reviewer for the daily ABC. Every year, since 1963, he collects his weekly essays under the title *Pensamiento español.* Madrid: Rialp. Fernández de la Mora's position is ultraconservative.

Ferrater Mora, José. "Dos obras maestras españolas." *Cuadernos* (París) 42, (1960), pp. 47-54. An excellent critical review of Laín Entralgo's major work: *La espera y la esperanza.*

Goytisolo, Juan. "L'Espagne et l'Europe." *Les Tempes Modernes,* Paris, (juillet, 1962).

Gullón, Ricardo. Gullón's observations in the series "Carta de España," are informative and perceptive evaluations of Spanish culture. They appeared in *Asonante,* Revista trimestral de la Universidad de Puerto Rico. Of special interest are the issues of octubre-diciembre, 1958, and enero-marzo, 1959.

*Insula* #224-225, 1965. Special issue dedicated to the Generation of 1936.

Jiménez Lozano, José. *Meditación española sobre la libertad religiosa.* Barcelona: Nova Terra, 1966. A searching essay on the role of the liberal Catholic intellectual in post-Civil War Spain.

Laín Entralgo, Pedro. *España como problema.* Madrid: Aguilar, 1962.

_____."Aranguren, humanista." *Cuadernos para el diálogo* (abril, 1966), pp. 27-28.

Mainer, José Carlos. "La revista *Escorial* en la vida literaria de su tiempo." *Insula,* #271 (junio, 1969); #275-6 (oct-nov., 1969). This study is appended to Mainer's recently published anthology of Falangist literature, *Falange y literatura.*Barcelona: Labor, 1971.

Mañach, Jorge. *Visitas españolas.* Madrid: Revista de Occidente, 1960. Interviews with Aranguren, Laín and others.

Marías, Julián. *Los españoles.* Madrid: Revista de Occidente, 1963. Essays on culture and the position of the Spanish intellectual under the Franco regime.

Marichal, Juan. *El nuevo pensamiento político español*. México: Finisterre, 1966.

Marrero, Vicente. *La guerra española y el trust de cerebros*. Madrid: Punta Europa, 1962. A totally tendentious piece of work but highly informative in regard to literary sources dealing directly with attitudes toward the Civil War.

Mermall, Thomas. "Concepts of Humanism in the Contemporary Spanish Essay." *Hispanic Review* (July, 1971), pp.237-48.

——————"En torno a 'Ideas y creencias': implicaciones de un concepto orteguiano en la ensayística de post guerra." *Hispanófila*, 43, 1971.

Montes, María José. *La guerra española en la creación literaria (ensayo bibliográfico)*. Anejos de Cuadernos Bibliográficos de la Guerra de España (1936-1939). Universidad de Madrid, 1970.

Ortuño, Manuel. "El Opus Dei." *Cuadernos Americanos* (enero-febrero, 1963), pp. 40-66.

Payne, Stanley. *Falange: A study of Spanish Fascism*. Stanford University Press, 1961.

Ridruejo, Dionisio. *En algunas ocasiones*. Madrid: Aguilar, 1960.

——————*Escrito en España*. Buenos Aires: Losada, 1962. These books are indispensable for an understanding of the liberal Falangist consciousness.

Rojas, Carlos. *Diálogos para otra España*. Barcelona: Ariel, 1966. A meditation on the theme of the "two Spains."

Sastre, Alfonso. *La revolución y la crítica de la cultura*. Barcelona: Grijalbo, 1970. An indictment of contemporary Spanish criticism of culture by one of Spain's leading dramatists.

Southworth, Herbert. *Antifalange*. Paris: Ruedo Ibérico, 1967. A Marxist view of the Falangist intellectuals.

Tierno Galván, Enrique. "Los intelectuales en la España contemporánea." *Puerto* (oct-dic., 1967), pp. 24-28.

*Symposium* #22, 1968. Special issue dedicated to the Generation of 1936.

*Triunfo*. Número especial (junio de 1972). *La cultura en la España del siglo XX*.

# General Bibliography.

In addition to the titles cited at the end of each chapter the following works were consulted:

Abellán José Luis. *Ortega en la filosofía española*. Madrid: Tecnos, 1966.

Adorno, Theodor W. *Intervenciones: Nueve modelos de crítica*. (Eingriffe, Neuen Kritische Modelle); (Trans. by R. J. Vernengo). Caracas, 1969.

Altizer, Thomas J. J. *Mircea Eliade and the Dialectic of the Sacred*. Philadelphia: The Westminster Press, 1963.

Aranguren, José L. *La ética de Ortega.* Madrid: Taurus, 1953.

_____ *Moral y sociedad.* Madrid: Cuadernos para el diálogo, 1965.

_____ *El marxismo como moral.* Madrid: Alianza Editorial, 1968.

Araya, Guillermo. *Claves filológicas para la comprensión de Ortega.* Madrid: Gredos, 1971.

Arendt, Hannah. *The Human Condition.* New York: Doubleday and Co., 1959.

_____ *Men in Dark Times.* New York: Harcourt, Brace & World, 1955.

_____ *The Origins of Totalitarianism.* New York: World Publishing Co., 1958.

Baker, Herschel. *The Image of Man: A Study of Human Dignity in Classical Antiquity, the Middle Ages and the Renaissance.* New York: Harper Torchbooks, 1961.

Barthes, Roland. *Writing Degree Zero. Elements of Semiology.* (Trans. by A. Levers and C. Smith). Preface by Susan Sontag. Boston: Beacon Press, 1970.

Benjamin, Walter. *Illuminations.* (Ed. and with an introduction by Hannah Arendt) New York: Schocken, 1969.

Blackham, H.J. *Six Existentialist Thinkers.* New York: Harper Torchbooks, 1952.

Burke, Kenneth. *The Rhetoric of Religion.* Berkeley: University of California Press, 1970.

_____ *Language as Symbolic Action.* Berkeley: University of California Press, 1966.

_____ *A Grammar of Motives.* Berkeley: University of California Press, 1962.

Cassirer, Ernst. *An Essay on Man.* New Haven: Yale University Press, 1962.

Carr, Raymond. *Spain 1808-1939.* Oxford: The Clarendon Press, 1966.

Díaz Plaja, Fernando. *La historia de España en sus documentos: el siglo XX (1923-1936).* Madrid: Instituto de Estudios Políticos, 1964.

Díaz Plaja, Guillermo. *Memorias de una generación destruida: 1930-1936.* Barcelona: Delos-Ayma, 1966.

Edie, James, et al. *Christianity and Existentialism.* Chicago: Northwestern University Press, 1963.

Ferrater Mora, José. *Diccionario de filosofía.* 2 tomos, quinta edición, Buenos Aires: Sudamericana, 1965.

Feuer, Lewis S. (ed.). *Basic Writings on Politics and Philosophy: Karl Marx and Friedrich Engels.* New York: Doubleday and Co., 1959.

Freud, Sigmund. *Civilization and Its Discontents.* (Trans. and ed. by James Strachey) New York: Norton, 1962.

_____ *The Ego and the Id.* (Trans. and ed. by James Strachey) New York: Norton, 1962.

_____ *Beyond the Pleasure Principle.* (Trans. by James Strachey) New York, Bantam Books, 1963.

_____ *The Future of an Illusion.* (Trans. by W.D. Robson-Scott) New York: Doubleday-Anchor (no date).

_____ *The History of the Psychoanalytic Movement,* in *The Basic*

*Writings of Sigmund Freud.* (A.A. Brill, trans. and ed.) New York: Modern Library, 1938.

Friedrich, Carl J. (ed.). *The Philosophy of Hegel.* New York: Modern Library, 1954.

Fromm, Erich (ed.). *Socialist Humanism: An International Symposium.* New York: Doubleday Anchor, 1966.

Garaudy, Roger. *Marxism in the Twentieth Century.* (Trans. by Rene Hague) New York: Scribner's Sons, 1970.

Ganivet, Angel. *Obras completas.* (2 tomos) Madrid: Aguilar, 1961.

Hegel, G.W.F. *The Phenomenology of Mind.* (Trans. by J.B. Baillie) New York: Harper Torchbooks, 1967.

Heidegger, Martin. *Being and Time.* (Trans. by J. Macquatie & E. Robinson) London: SCM Press Ltd., 1962.

——————.*An Introduction to Metaphysics.* (Trans. by Ralph Manheim) New Haven: Yale University Press, 1959.

Hughes, H. Stuart. *Consciousness and Society: The Reorientation of European Social Thought 1890-1930.* New York: Random House, 1958.

Jackson, Gabriel. *The Spanish Republic and the Civil War: 1931-1939.* Princeton University Press, 1965.

Jung, Carl Gustav. *Four Archetypes.* (Trans. by F.C. Hull) Princeton: Bollingen Series, 1969.

Kierkegaard, Soren. *Fear and Trembling. The Sickness unto Death.* (Trans. by W. Lowrie) New York: Doubleday Anchor, 1954.

Koestler, Arthur. *The Ghost in the Machine.* Chicago: Gateway, 1971.

Laín Entralgo, Pedro. *Teoría y realidad del otro.* (2 tomos) Madrid: Revista de Occidente, 1961.

Lichtheim, George. *A Short History of Socialism.* New York: Praeger, 1970.

Lubac, Henri de, S.J. *The Drama of Atheist Humanism.* (Trans. by Edith M. Rileg) Cleveland: The World Publishing Company, 1963.

Man, Paul de. *Blindness and Insight: Essays in the Rhetoric of Contemporary Criticism.* New York: Oxford University Press, 1971.

Mannheim, Karl. *Ideology and Utopia.* (Trans. by L. Wirth and E. Shils) New York: Harcourt Brace & World (Harvest Paperback, no date).

Maravall, José Antonio. *Antiguos y modernos: La idea de progreso en el desarrollo inicial de una sociedad.* Madrid: Sociedad de Estudios y Publicaciones, 1966.

Marcuse, Herbert. *Eros and Civilization.* New York: Random House, 1962.

Marías, Julián. *Obras.* Madrid: Revista de Occidente, 1961. *La estructura social,* VI; *El método histórico de las generaciones,* VI.

——————.*Ortega: Circunstancia y vocación.* Madrid: Revista de Occidente, 1960.

Marx, Karl and Frederick Engels. *The German Ideology.* New York: International Publishers, 1960.

Ortega y Gasset, José. *Obras completas.* Revista de Occidente, 1964. *En torno a Galileo,* V; *Ideas y creencias,* V; *Historia como sistema,* VI; *Prólogo para alemanes,* VIII.

Pegis, Anton C. (ed.) *Introduction to Saint Thomas Aquinas.* New York: Modern Library, 1948.

Rico, Francisco. *El pequeño mundo del hombre: Varia fortuna de una idea en las letras españolas*. Madrid: Castalia, 1970.

Richards, I.A. *The Philosophy of Rhetoric*. New York: Oxford University Press, 1966.

Sartre, Jean Paul. *Being and Nothingness: An Essay on Phenomenological Ontology*. (Trans. and with and introduction by Hazel Barnes) New York: Philosophical Library, 1956.

_____. *Les Mots*. Paris: Gallimard, 1964.

Unamuno, Miguel de. *Ensayos* (2 tomos). Madrid: Aguilar, 1970. *La agonía del cristianismo*, I; *Del sentimiento trágico de la vida*, II.

Wyss, Dieter. *Depth Psychology: A Critical History*. (Trans. by Gerald Onn) New York: W.W. Norton, 1966.

Zaner, Richard M. *The Way of Phenomenology: Criticism as a Philosophical Discipline*. New York: Pegasus, 1970.

Thomas Mermall, associate professor of Spanish at Brooklyn College of the City University of New York, specializes in the contemporary Hispanic essay. He has published articles in *Bulletin of Hispanic Studies, Cuadernos Americanos, Cuadernos Hispanoamericanos, Hispania, Hispanic Review, Hispanófila, Insula, Papeles de Son Armadans,* and *Thought.* He participated in the York College Colloquium on Contemporary Methods of Literary Analysis as Applied to Hispanic Literature and his contribution appears in the 1975 publication of the proceedings.

** bp** *Bilingual Press*
*Edi* **2 0 5 3** *güe*